SMALL-BOAT
SAILING

A Complete Guide

Sports Illustrated Winner's Circle Books

BOOKS ON TEAM SPORTS

Baseball
Basketball
Football: Winning Defense
Football: Winning Offense
Hockey
Lacrosse
Pitching
Soccer

BOOKS ON INDIVIDUAL SPORTS

Bowling
Competitive Swimming
Cross-Country Skiing
Figure Skating
Golf
Racquetball
Running for Women
Skiing
Tennis
Track: Championship Running
Track: Field Events

SPECIAL BOOKS

Backpacking
Canoeing
Fly Fishing
Scuba Diving
Small-Boat Sailing
Strength Training

SMALL-BOAT SAILING

A Complete Guide

by David Dellenbaugh and
Brad Dellenbaugh

Photography by Christopher Cunningham

Sports Illustrated
Winner's Circle Books
New York

Picture credits: Pages 91 (top, middle), 119 (top), 158 by Tom Ettinger; 112 by Robert D. Hagan; 31 (top), 42, 44, 45, 46, 56, 63, 169, 197, 198-199, 204-205, 206-207 by Bill Jaspersohn; 13 courtesy Mystic Seaport Museum, Mystic, Connecticut; 111, 191 by Dan Nerney; 14 (top) courtesy David Dellenbaugh. All diagrams by Brad Dellenbaugh. All other photographs by Christopher Cunningham.

FIRST EDITION

Designer: *Kim Llewellyn*

Library of Congress Cataloging-in-Publication Data

Dellenbaugh, David.
  Sports illustrated small-boat sailing: a complete guide/by
David Dellenbaugh and Brad Dellenbaugh; photography by Christopher
Cunningham.—1st ed.
    p. cm.—(Sports illustrated winner's circle books)
  ISBN 0-452-26272-0
  1. Sailing. 2. Sailing—Equipment and supplies. I. Dellenbaugh,
Brad. II. Title. III. Series.
GV811.D42 1990
797.1'24—dc19   90 91 92 93 94 AG/HL 10 9 8 7 6 5 4 3 2 1   90-6053

Contents

SMALL-BOAT
SAILING
A Complete Guide

1

Sailing Today

Around dinnertime on September 26, 1983, the sky over Newport, Rhode Island, was turning from dark blue to black. Along the waterfront, thousands of sailors and spectators crowded the docks to catch a glimpse of *Australia II.* The Australian crew had just won the seventh race of the America's Cup, and that meant they had broken the longest winning streak in sports history.

The key to the Australians' come-from-behind victory was a controversial winged keel that had been kept under wraps during the long Cup campaign. That evening, however, as *Australia II* was hoisted out of the water, the protective shroud was left open. For the first time, the public saw her awesome blue and white keel, glistening as the cameras flashed. As the throngs cheered, few realized how great an impact that oddly shaped piece of lead would have on the future of sailing.

Of course, the Australians' victory meant that the silver America's Cup would leave the New York Yacht Club and head for Perth. But more than that, it helped usher the entire sport of sailing into a new era. With the Cup now up for grabs, more countries than ever entered the 1987 America's Cup. The ensuing series became a global sensation, and when *Stars & Stripes* finally trounced *Kookaburra,* the races were viewed by a worldwide television audience.

This unprecedented media attention introduced sailing to millions of new spectators. It paved the way for more television coverage of sailing, increased commercial sponsorship in the sport, and creation of the first professional racing circuits. In short, the America's Cup captured and communicated, better than ever before, the excitement of sailing at every level.

Today more than 11 million Americans are involved in sailing. Despite the cost of owning a boat and the problem of finding access to the water, the sport

With 11 million participants nationwide, sailing is one of America's fastest-growing sports.

is growing faster than almost any other. As this book will show you, it's a great time to get started in sailing—thanks, in part, to an innovative winged keel that came from the land Down Under.

THE EVOLUTION OF SAILING

Sailing wasn't always such a dynamic sport. In fact, for most of its history, sailing has not been a sport at all, but a means of conducting commerce and war. It wasn't until the early 1800s that sailing started to evolve as a recreational activity among the well-to-do. The most famous pleasure sailboat of the 19th century was undoubtedly the schooner *America,* which sailed across the Atlantic in 1851 and won a huge silver trophy called the Hundred Guineas Cup. That, of course, was the beginning of the Americans' 132-year domination of the America's Cup.

For the next century, sailing remained largely the province of the wealthy. Sailors wore blazers and white pants, and hired deckhands to do the hard work on their yachts. One important exception was a group of smaller boats, including sandbaggers, catboats, and sailing canoes, that began racing and sailing during the latter part of the 19th century. These were the ancestors of today's small sailboats, and they gained popularity around the country.

By the middle of the 20th century, sailing began to evolve much more rapidly. The introduction of fiberglass hulls, for example, was to boats what the production line had been to cars. No longer did every hull have to be custom-built out of wood. Now boats could be popped out of molds, and this meant they were less expensive, more rugged, and easier to maintain.

Another major boon for sailing was the introduction and proliferation of off-the-beach boats in the 1950s, '60s, and '70s. These included multihulls like the Aqua Cat and Hobie Cat as well as "board" boats like the Sunfish and Laser. These boats were inexpensive, easy to transport, and because they could be launched right off the beach, they made the sport accessible to a large new group of people outside yacht club circles. The boats were also fun to sail and very sensitive, which made them great for learning and for introducing people to the sport.

By the 1980s, the generation that had grown up on off-the-beach boats was ready for a larger commitment to sailing. Thus began the growth of small cruising boats that were affordable, easy to tow behind a car, and raceable. The J/24, introduced in 1979, was a perfect example. This 24-footer had two bunks below and was used widely for one-design racing (against other boats that were

In the early days of the sport, recreational sailing was largely the province of the wealthy.

exactly the same). Within five years of its debut, more than 3,000 boats had been sold around the world.

While many Laser sailors moved on to bigger boats, some headed in the opposite direction. In the mid-'70s, a strange type of craft started appearing on beaches and in harbors around North America. It looked like a surfboard but had a sail, and it was called a Windsurfer, or sailboard. Sailboards turned the sailing experience into a natural extension of the sailor's body. They offered the epitome of fun, fast, inexpensive, and transportable sailing. After a slow start in North America, the boardsailing craze caught fire in less-conservative Europe and grew rapidly around the rest of the world during the next decade.

Small Sailboats

Small sailboats like the Sunfish (top left), the Laser II (lower left), and the multihulled Hobie Cat (upper right) have all made learning to sail easier and more affordable. The advent of small keelboats like the J/24 (lower right) has expanded sailing's dimensions even more.

Today there are more ways to go sailing than ever before. This is one of the unique and attractive facets of the sport: Whether you are looking for speed, adventure, or pure relaxation, there is a boat and a group of sailors that are perfect for you.

Day sailing: By far the most popular method of sailing is simply to jump into a boat and go out for a morning or afternoon (or both) sail. There's nothing quite as relaxing as being on the water in a sailboat with no particular goal in mind except to have a good time. When day sailing is your preference, almost any kind of boat will do, from a 14-foot Laser to a 40-foot cruising boat.

Overnight cruising: If day sailing is like hiking, then overnight cruising is the equivalent of camping. When you have a large enough boat and a destination, you are ready to spend the night afloat. This is one of the most popular pastimes of experienced sailors and their families. On a Saturday evening in the summer, you don't have to go any farther than the nearest sheltered harbor to find cruising boats at anchor, with sailors relaxing and enjoying themselves after a fun day of sailing.

One-design racing: For competitive spirits, sailing offers one-design and handicap racing. One-design boats are, in theory, exactly the same. The thrill of one-design racing is that it's primarily a contest of sailing ability, rather than a test of who has the best boat (or the most money). It's also great because you're racing one-on-one with the rest of the fleet, and the first boat across the finish line wins. Most one-design races are for boats that are less than 30 feet long, with centerboards or keels, and have open cockpits.

Handicap racing: Boats that get together for a race are often not identical, especially if they are larger boats with cabins. Many races, in fact, feature diverse groups of boats racing against each other on handicap. It's a bit like golfing—every boat is assigned a rating based on either the boat's measurements or its past performance. During a race, this rating translates into a time allowance. The advantage of handicapping is that it allows a diverse group of boats to compete against one another. The disadvantages are that it's difficult to come up with fair handicaps and it's hard to know how you are doing on the course, since the last boat across the finish line may win the race.

Sailboards: As we mentioned earlier, boardsailing has been the most explosive area of sailing during the past decade. The reason is that it's fun, fast, and relatively inexpensive. Finding a place to launch a sailboard is also easier. The term "boardsailing" covers a wide range of activities from the thrill of wave jumping in Maui to the intense one-design competition of the Olympics. In fact,

The pleasures of small-boat sailing can include everything from day sailing (above), to overnight cruising, to racing (below).

the world speed-sailing record of more than 40 knots (about 47 miles per hour) is currently held by a sailboard. Because sailboards are quite different from other small boats, we will not cover them in this book. For more information, we recommend *Sports Illustrated Boardsailing* by Major Hall.

Multihulls: Another unique breed of sailing craft is the boat with more than one hull. In a wide variety of racing conditions, including the 1988 America's Cup, catamarans (two hulls) and trimarans (three hulls) have proved themselves to be the fastest all-around racing craft in the world. Besides their exhilarating speed, multihulls have many desirable qualities, especially for beginning sailors. They are easily launched off the beach, and their wide platform makes for a stable ride. While we don't refer specifically to multihulls in this book, much of what we say here can apply to sailing them.

THE LURE OF WIND AND WATER

Variety is only one of many reasons why people go sailing. Another reason is aesthetics. From the solitude of Thoreau's Walden Pond to the beauty of a Pacific sunset, there has always been something very alluring about the water. Perhaps it is the million different patterns and colors created by the wind, water, and sky. Or the reassuring sound of waves lapping at the shore or against the sides of a boat.

In a survey done a few years ago, thousands of people across the country were asked why they participated in their favorite outdoor activities. The following were their most popular responses (in order):

1. To enjoy nature and the outdoors.
2. To get exercise or keep in shape.
3. To get away from day-to-day problems.
4. To be with family and friends.
5. To have peace and quiet.

It's amazing how closely these answers describe the reasons why people go sailing. No matter what type of boat you sail, you'll have a great opportunity to experience the outdoors, relax, find peacefulness, and have a good time with other people. It's no wonder the sport is growing, as we try to find respite from our fast-paced world.

Believe it or not, sailing also offers great opportunities to stay in shape. Just ask anyone who has hiked (used their weight to keep the boat flat) for several hours in a Laser, helped grind the genoa winches on a 40-footer, or sailed across the Atlantic. Like the athletes in other sports, top sailors must be physically fit. Most sailing activities don't have excessive athletic requirements. In fact, one of the reasons why sailing is so popular is that it can be enjoyed by people of all ages and physical abilities.

Consider the example of the "Great Dane," Paul Elvstrom, who is regarded by many as the greatest sailor of all time. Elvstrom won the first of his four sailing gold medals in 1948. Forty years later, he competed in his seventh Olympic Games for Denmark, with his daughter Trine as crew. They finished not too far out of the medal hunt.

THE GOALS OF THIS BOOK

With most sports, there is a strong relationship between knowledge and enjoyment. In other words, the more you understand how to play a game, the more fun you will have. This is certainly true with sailing. In fact, since sailing has more mental aspects than, perhaps, any other sport, understanding what you are doing is particularly important.

That is why we have written this book. Our goal is to help you enjoy sailing as much as possible. In order to do this, we hope to teach you how to handle a small boat skillfully. If you are able to sail a boat wherever you want, and do so safely, then you will realize the greatest rewards from the sport.

There's one thing we should make clear from the beginning: We believe in teaching *performance*. When you're sailing, performance means being able to get the most out of the boat and out of yourself. Of course, we are not saying you should be going for maximum speed all the time (we'll leave that for the hard-core racers). What we are saying is that you will have much more fun if you know how to achieve performance whenever you want.

The concept of performance has been important ever since people took to the water with sails. When moving cargo, for example, time was money. In military affairs, sailing performance was a matter of life and death. For recreational sailing, performance has slightly different purposes. In racing, obviously, the goal is to get around the course as fast as possible. In day sailing or cruising, performance means many things: sailing upwind efficiently; reaching your destination before dark; sailing instead of paddling or turning on the engine; experiencing the thrill of speed downwind; and feeling good about realizing your boat's potential.

We believe that everyone learning the sport should learn how to sail the "right" way—which will give you more options and more enjoyment in the long

If you learn to sail efficiently, your time on the water will be safer and more fun.

run. To that end, we will explain not only the "hows" but also the "whys" of sailing. We'll begin, in Chapter 2, with the most important element for sailors to understand—the wind. Then, in subsequent chapters, we'll teach you the language of sailing, the basics of getting started, how to sail upwind and downwind, how to get the most out of your sails, sailing's rules of the road, how to read the weather, safe sailing, and how to get started in racing. Finally, in Chapter 13 we'll discuss how you can take the next step and get more involved in the sport.

Sailing, for both of us, has been a lifetime sport, pastime, recreation, and avocation. It can be all those things for you, too, once you understand the basics.

A final note: As much as possible, we have tried to write this book in the first person plural: *we*. However, from time to time, Dave has thrown in an anecdote from his own experience. Thus, whenever you see an "I" in the book, think "Dave."

2

Understanding the Wind

Billowing smoke. Swirling dust and sand. Dancing leaves. Pinwheels, flags, windmills, kites. Ocean waves, sand dunes, and snowdrifts. The wind is invisible, yet we can feel it all around us and see its effects. It is chilling in winter, a welcome refreshment in summer, and potentially destructive almost anytime.

There is no better place to experience the wind than out on the water, in a small sailboat. By definition, a sailboat exists because of the wind. It gathers all of its life from the breeze and is helpless when the wind disappears. Sailors put up sails to harvest the energy of the wind, and they take down sails when they are overpowered by its awesome force.

My first Bermuda Race, in 1972, was a good demonstration of the wind's many attitudes. Two days out of Newport, we were becalmed in the middle of the meandering Gulf Stream. I remember staring incredulously at an ocean as calm as a pond at dusk. We even went swimming! Twenty-four hours later, we sailed into a near-hurricane, with winds over 50 knots. The millpond had turned into a maelstrom, and we were slamming off the backs of 20-foot waves. The contrast was incredible.

Whether racing or day sailing, getting tuned in to the wind is probably the most important thing a sailor can do. In fact, you must feel comfortable with the wind before you'll ever feel in control of your boat.

In sailing, there are two aspects of the wind that are important: strength and direction. Before heading out on the water, try to get a good feel for both of these variables. You won't want to go sailing, for example, if gale force winds are expected; this wouldn't help your enjoyment of the sport. You might also want to avoid sailing in a strong *offshore* breeze (a breeze blowing away from the shore) until you're confident of your ability to sail upwind—unless,

Learning to use available wind to your advantage is a key to sailing well.

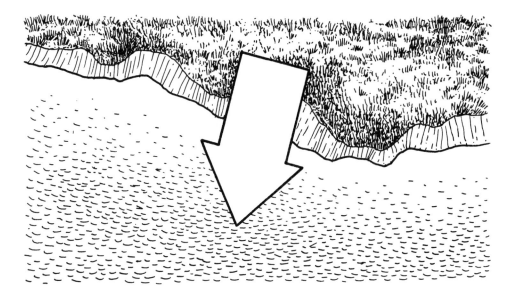

Offshore breeze.
An offshore breeze blows from the land onto the water. It is usually a warm breeze affording fairly calm water conditions, but you should be careful about sailing too far away from land in an offshore breeze: if you're not proficient at sailing upwind, you may never get home.

of course, you've always wanted to make that 10-mile trip to the other side of the bay.

There are several ways to get an idea of wind strength and direction before you head out on the water. The first is simply your own observation. As author Dave Perry once said, "When I wake up and see my mailbox blowing sideways, I get a sudden urge to mow the lawn." The British have come up with a system of estimating wind strength on land, called the Beaufort scale. It offers a good method for judging how hard it's blowing by looking at the activity of the trees, but you have to be careful that you don't underestimate the wind. There will usually be more breeze out on the water than in the shelter of your backyard.

Another way to get an idea of wind strength and direction is by listening

The Beaufort Scale

Named after Sir Francis Beaufort, who developed it, the Beaufort Scale indicates wind force by a series of numbers from 0 to 17. You can learn to gauge wind speeds by observing the effect of the wind on water and land, as charted below.

Beaufort (Force) Number	MPH	Knots	Name	Appearance of land and water
0	Under 1	Under 1	Calm	Smoke rises vertically; water calm, mirrorlike
1	1–3	1–3	Light air	Wind direction shown by smoke but not by weathervanes; ripples on water
2	4–7	4–6	Light breeze	Leaves rustle; wind felt on face; weathervanes moved by wind; small wavelets on water
3	8–12	7–10	Gentle breeze	Leaves and twigs in constant motion; wind causes flags to flutter; large wavelets, scattered whitecaps on water
4	13–18	11–16	Moderate breeze	Wind raises dust and loose paper; small branches are moved; small waves, many whitecaps on water
5	19–24	17–21	Fresh breeze	Small leafed trees begin to sway; moderate waves, whitecaps, some spray on water
6	25–31	22–27	Strong breeze	Large branches in motion; phone lines whistle; umbrellas used with difficulty; large waves, whitecaps everywhere, spray on water
7	32–38	28–33	Moderate gale	Whole trees in motion; difficult to walk against wind; sea heaps, white foam blows in streaks
8	39–46	34–40	Fresh gale	Wind breaks twigs off trees; walking impeded; waves long with well-marked white streaks on surface
9	47–54	41–47	Strong gale	Slight structural damage to buildings occurs; shingles torn off roofs; high waves, rolling seas, streaks everywhere, reduced visibility due to heavy spray
10	55–63	48–55	Whole gale	Trees uprooted; considerable structural damage to buildings; extremely high waves with overhanging crests; reduced visibility
11	64–72	56–64	Storm	Widespread damage; find secure shelter!
12–17			Hurricane	Devastation

to the weather report on your local radio station. Don't put too much faith in these predictions, however, since they're often generalizations bearing little resemblance to reality. When we were kids, the local weatherman used to broadcast from his station's airplane while flying over Long Island Sound. We'd be sitting in our boats, totally becalmed, when out of our radios would come a report that the wind was blowing 15 to 20 knots from the south. We used to joke that the weatherman was holding his anemometer out the window of the plane.

A more reliable source of wind and weather predictions is the National Oceanographic and Atmospheric Agency (NOAA), which broadcasts continuous weather updates on special frequencies. They provide information such as: "Winds will be south to southwest this morning, at 5 to 10 knots, shifting to westerly this afternoon and building to 15 to 20. Wave heights 1 to 3 feet on the bay, 3 to 6 feet on the ocean. Small-craft advisories will be in effect this afternoon, and small-craft warnings should be heeded after 5:00 tonight. High tide at Long Point at 1:14 P.M." This is the kind of information that anyone heading out for a sail really needs to know. (Chapter 10 will cover wind and weather predictions in more depth.)

Once you've decided that conditions are satisfactory for sailing, it's time to head out on the water. Here it will be easier to gauge wind direction and strength because you are not shielded by trees or buildings, and you can see the wind on the water.

WIND DIRECTION

An experienced sailor knows the wind direction at all times. This information is very important for trimming your sails and handling your boat properly. When we talk about wind direction, we mean where the wind is blowing *from* (not where it's going *to*). There are a number of ways to determine this.

When we learned to sail, we were taught a method known to old salts as "holding a finger to the wind." To do this, put your forefinger in the water (or in your mouth) to get it wet and then hold it up in the wind. Wherever you feel the greatest chill on your finger is where the wind is coming from. Neither of us has used this method too recently, but it still works.

A more reliable guide, for both wind direction and strength, is simply the feel of the wind on your body. America's Cup skipper Dennis Conner reportedly gets his hair cut very short before major regattas so that he'll be able to feel the wind on the back of his neck. This way he can sense a change in wind direction or strength without having to look around all the time.

Since we're not all quite as intuitive as Dennis Conner, we need a few visual clues to help us determine wind direction. Our personal method of choice is to use the ripples on the water. Look toward the wind and try to direct your line of sight so that it bisects the ripples (is in line with the direction they're moving). Sometimes you can stick your arm out straight toward the wind at the same time, and move it until it is perpendicular to the ripples. Then you are pointing at the wind.

I remember iceboating for the first time a couple of years ago. Until then, I never could figure out how iceboaters knew what the wind was doing. It seemed that, without ripples on the water, the wind was truly invisible. I found I was right to a certain extent, but I learned that I could tell a lot about the wind by feeling what it was doing to my boat. This sense of feel is extremely important in sailing.

There are, of course, many other ways to figure out the wind direction. You can look at flags (on land or on boats) or at smoke coming out of a smokestack. Other indicators are telltales (short pieces of yarn) tied to your boat's rigging, and a masthead "fly" (a kind of wind vane) on top of your mast. Some bigger boats even have instruments, connected to the masthead unit, that give a continuous readout on wind direction and velocity. Unfortunately that's a luxury you probably won't ever find on a small boat.

A more scientific way to tell wind direction is to let your sails luff (flap in the wind). Just let the sheets (the lines used to pull in the sails) go for a few seconds. The sails will start flapping and will move to a position that is lined up with the flow of the wind. If you look where the sails are pointing, that's where the wind is coming from.

One refinement of this technique is to let the sails flap and then turn your boat so the sails are luffing along its centerline. Now the bow of your boat is pointing toward the wind. This technique is often used by racing sailors when they are trying to find the wind direction before the start of a race.

One of the hardest times to tell wind direction is when the wind is so light that you can't see any ripples on the water. Some racing sailors light up a cigarette so they can watch where the smoke goes. We like the idea of blowing soap bubbles and watching where they float. When the bubbles hover in your cockpit, you know you've got a real drifter on your hands!

Wind Direction

An excellent way to judge wind direction is to look at the angle of the wind ripples on the water. When your gaze is perpendicular to most of the ripples, you are looking directly into the wind.

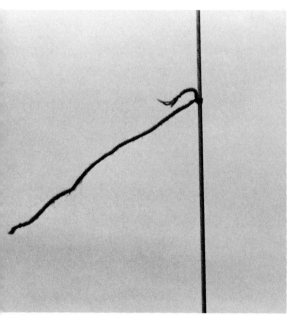

A telltale—a piece of yarn tied to your a shroud or sail—is another useful device for figuring wind direction.

No telltale handy? Then look for a flapping flag . . .

. . . or at your masthead fly. This wind vane, located at the top of the mast, is very accurate.

WIND

If you let your sails luff in the breeze, they will line up with the direction of the wind.

Finally, you can determine wind direction by using your boat as a giant wind vane. Turn the boat so the sails are luffing right in the middle of the boat. Your bow is now pointed into the wind.

WIND STRENGTH

Knowing (and being able to anticipate) the strength of the wind is very important for both safety and performance. When I was 14, I was sailing my 13-foot
Blue Jay home from a race when we were suddenly caught in a 40-knot squall.
At that age, I didn't know the wind could blow so hard or that it could come
up so suddenly. We capsized immediately and spent 30 long minutes in the
water before we were rescued.

It's very important to know when a squall is coming or when the wind is
about to die for the evening (and make you paddle home). Here are some useful
rules of thumb.

• The key to anticipating the strength of the wind coming toward you is
the appearance of ripples on the water. (Don't confuse the larger wave pattern
with the tiny wavelets created by the wind.) Basically, the closer together the
ripples are, the more wind there is.

• Another sign is the color of the water surface. The darker the water, the
more wind there is (because when there are a lot of wind ripples, less of the
sky's brightness is reflected). You can often see puffs of wind as dark blotches
moving across the water.

• If you're looking *toward* the sun, the glare will make it look as if there's
more wind than if you're looking *away from* the sun. Also, the breeze appears
stronger when you look toward the wind than when you look away from it. This
is because the back sides of the ripples are less steep and therefore reflect more
of the light-colored sky.

• When whitecaps begin to form on top of the waves (in an open body of
water), the wind is blowing about 12 or 13 knots. Most small boats begin to
get quite tippy around this velocity.

• Other good guides for wind strength are the action of smoke coming out
of smokestacks, how straight flags are blowing, and how much other sailboats
are heeled (tipped to one side).

In the United States, the National Weather Service, a branch of the
NOAA, uses a system of signals to warn sailors about high winds and storms.
For example, if you see a triangular red flag on the flagpole at your local marina
or yacht club, a small-craft warning has been posted. This means that wind and
sea conditions are such that small boats should not go out. Other signals warn
of gale winds and hurricanes. You should definitely know what these signals
mean and where they are displayed in your area.

Wind speeds, by the way, like boat speeds, are almost always measured in

Wind Strength

The ripples on the water are your best guide to both wind strength and wind direction. Yet another clue to wind direction: seagulls, which usually stand facing into the wind.

As this boat's sails luff to find the wind direction, whitecaps are just beginning to form, meaning the wind velocity is about 13 knots.

knots. A knot is defined as one nautical mile per hour. A nautical mile is 6,080 feet, or 14 percent longer than a statute mile (5,280 feet). Thus, if the wind velocity is 20 knots, it is blowing about 23 miles per hour.

TRUE VS. APPARENT WIND

There is another factor affecting wind strength and direction that we haven't mentioned yet. It has to do with the wind caused by your boat moving through the water. Let's go back for a minute to the meteorologist who held his ane-mometer out the window of the plane. Even though the boats below had no breeze, he really did feel a strong wind from the south. The reason is that the plane was flying fast in a southerly direction. It's like putting your hand out the window of your car when you're driving on the interstate. You'll feel a 60-mile-an-hour breeze.

The breeze you feel from a moving plane or car is called the "apparent" wind. It works the same for boats, although the effect is less pronounced. Say you are standing on the end of a dock and the wind you feel is 9 knots from the north. This is called the "true" wind. Now I come sailing by you at 4 knots, heading east. The instruments on my boat say the wind I feel is blowing 10 knots from the northeast. This is my apparent wind; it's a combination of the true wind, which you feel, and the wind caused by my boat moving through the water.

When sailing upwind (into the wind), your apparent wind will be greater than the true wind; when you're sailing downwind (with the wind behind you), it will be less. As long as the boat is moving forward, the direction of your apparent wind will be shifted more toward your bow than the true wind. As a sailor, you should be concerned primarily with the apparent wind, because this is the wind in which you sail and it determines how you must trim your sails. That's why it's o.k. to use telltales and a masthead fly (both of which indicate apparent wind) to determine wind direction.

Whether you're a racer or day sailor, not knowing the wind strength and direction is like driving blindfolded. If you take off the blindfold, suddenly you can predict the sharp turns and give a little more gas before the hills. You'll know where to point your boat and how far in to pull the sails. It's important to keep trying to understand the wind no matter what else you do. This will make learning the sport and controlling your boat much easier.

True vs. Apparent Wind

There can be a big difference between the true wind (felt on land or on a stationary boat) and the apparent wind (felt on a moving object).

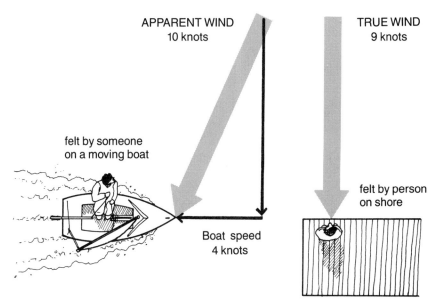

The apparent wind you feel on a moving boat is a vector sum involving both the magnitude and the direction of the wind created by the boat's movement and the true wind as felt by an observer on shore.

HOW THE WIND MAKES
A SAILBOAT GO

Sailboats are machines that harness the wind for their power. It's easy to understand how the wind can push a boat along with it, but a lot more difficult to figure out how a boat can actually make progress into the wind. It's a little like trying to comprehend how airplanes ever get off the ground.

When we were young aspiring sailors, we used to build crude model boats consisting of a rectangular piece of wood for a hull, with some sort of stick mast and a square sail made from an old rag. Our test area was usually the neighbor's pond, and we quickly learned one thing: the boat sailed in only one direction—downwind. This meant we could launch it only from the upwind side of the pond.

The ancient sailors faced similar problems. Though they angled their sails to catch the wind and used a paddle to steer, they still had a hard time going anywhere except with the wind. Their eventual solution was a flat board that acted as a kind of brake. They put this board down into the water alongside the boat to keep it from moving sideways.

Today this flat board is called a *keel* or *centerboard,* and it's the secret to how a boat can sail into the wind. To imagine how it works, think about squeezing a slippery watermelon seed. When you put pressure on both sides of the seed, it usually squirts in a direction that's perpendicular to the forces.

With a sailboat, the wind is pushing the sails on one side while the water pushes the centerboard, rudder, and hull on the other side. As the boat is squeezed by these two forces, it "squirts" forward and is thus able to sail upwind. There are, of course, many more complicated aerodynamic and hydro-dynamic reasons why this works, but the important thing to know is that without your keel or centerboard you could not sail toward the wind.

How the Wind Makes a Sailboat Go

The ancient sailors could not sail upwind; they went downwind wherever the wind took them.

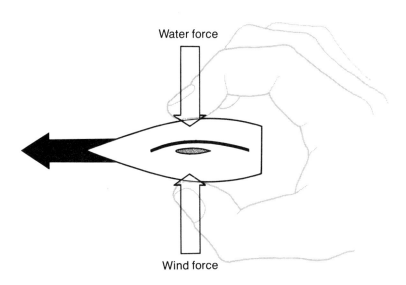

A boat sailing upwind is a little like a watermelon seed being squeezed between your fingers. With the wind pushing on one side of the sails and the water pushing on the other side of the centerboard, the boat moves forward.

Daggerboards, Centerboards, Keels

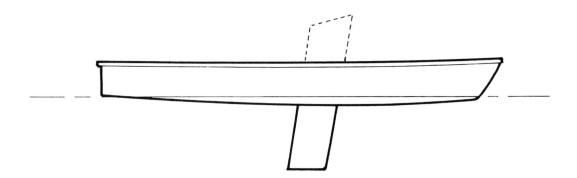

A **daggerboard** slides up and down through a slot in the center of the boat.

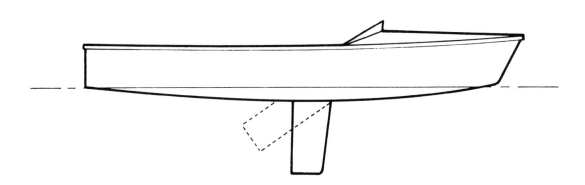

A **centerboard** pivots on a pin in the center of the boat.

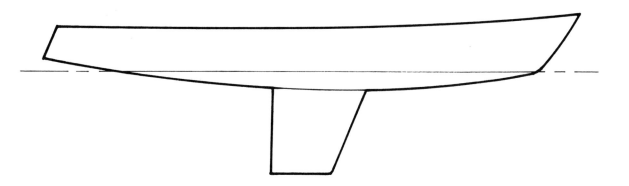

A **keel** is a heavy hydrofoil that sticks down under a boat, helping the boat sail to windward and reducing heel.

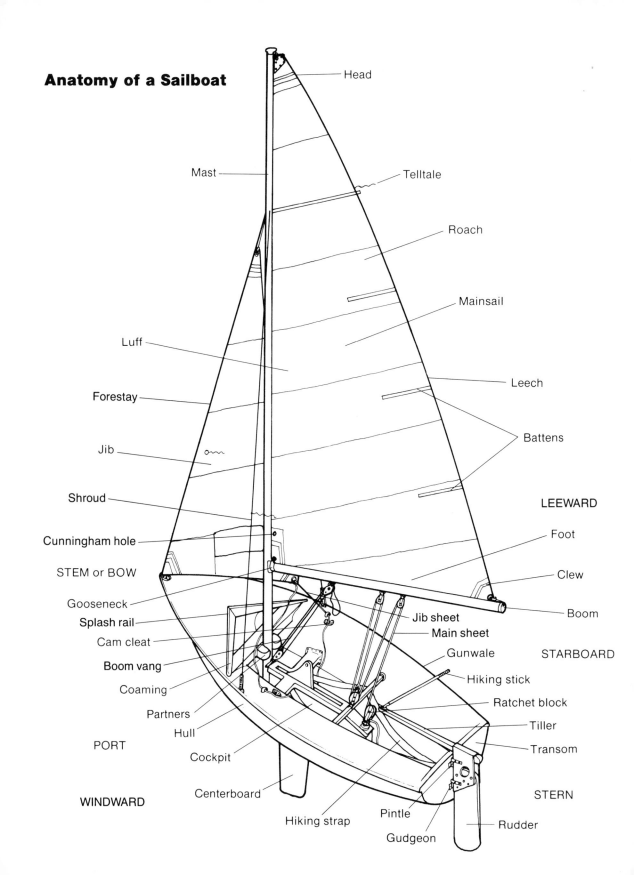

Anatomy of a Sailboat

Head

Mast

Telltale

Roach

Mainsail

Luff

Leech

Forestay

Battens

Jib

LEEWARD

Shroud

Foot

Cunningham hole

Clew

STEM or BOW

Boom

Gooseneck

Jib sheet

Splash rail

Main sheet

Cam cleat

STARBOARD

Boom vang

Gunwale

Coaming

Hiking stick

Partners

Ratchet block

Hull

Tiller

PORT

Transom

Cockpit

STERN

Centerboard

WINDWARD

Pintle

Hiking strap

Rudder

Gudgeon

3

The Language of Sailing

Perhaps more than any other sport, sailing has its own language. Being on a boat or around a group of sailors can often seem like visiting a foreign country. Rope is called "line," a pulley is a "block," the front of the boat is the "bow," and on it goes. While it's not critical to learn all the different terms immediately, it's good to know some of the basics. This will make life a lot easier when you get into the actual mechanics of sailing.

We've written this chapter as a sort of "Berlitz" for beginning sailors. Read through it now, and then use it as a reference whenever you hear or read a term you don't know. There's also an extensive glossary at the back of the book.

BASIC TERMINOLOGY

When you want to learn a foreign language, the best approach is to go live in a country where it is spoken. For aspiring sailors, the best way to learn all the proper terms is to spend time in a boat with an "old salt" (experienced sailor).

If you don't know any old salts (or if you want to brush up on your vocabulary before you go sailing with one), here is a brief list of the most common sailing terms.

Bow: the pointy end of the boat, the front.

Stern: the back end of the boat.

Forward: toward the bow of the boat.

Aft: toward the stern of the boat.

Port: the left side of the boat (facing forward).

39

Starboard: the right side of the boat (facing forward). Note that the port and starboard sides of a boat always stay the same, no matter which way you are facing.

Tack: the direction a boat is sailing in relation to the wind. The boat is on *starboard tack* if the wind is coming from the starboard side; on *port tack* if the wind is coming from the port side. The boat is always on the tack that's opposite the side the mainsail is on. For example, if the mainsail is on the starboard side, the boat is said to be on "port tack."

Tacking: the process of going from one tack to the other when the bow swings through the wind direction. Your sails will always luff (flap) during a tack.

Jibing: the process of going from one tack to another when the stern swings through the wind direction. When jibing, the boom often swings quickly from one side to the other, so you have to watch your head (also the word for a nautical toilet).

Leeward: away from the wind, or downwind. When the boat is under sail, the mainsail is always on the leeward side. When two boats are sailing in close proximity, the leeward boat is the one farther away from the wind.

Windward: toward the wind, or upwind. This is the opposite of leeward.

Hull

The *hull* is the body of the boat. Most small sailboats today are made of fiberglass or wood. Parts of the hull include:

Topsides: the sides of the boat above the waterline.

Waterline: the line where the hull intersects the surface of the water, sometimes indicated with a stripe or a change in paint color.

Bottom: the part of the hull below the waterline.

Transom: the flat surface at the stern.

Stem: the point where the topsides meet at the bow.

Deck

The *deck* is the walking platform that extends across the hull of a boat. Some boats, such as Thistles, have no deck; others, such as Lasers, are almost all deck.

Deck terms include:

Cockpit: the area cut out of the deck where you sit to sail the boat. With fiberglass construction, this is usually molded into the same piece as the deck.

Splash rail: a V-shaped rail located on the deck in front of the mast. It's designed to keep you dry by diverting waves that wash over the bow. When we sailed 12-Meters in the very rough waters off Perth, Australia, a splash rail was important to keep the boat from filling up with water.

Coaming: a low rail around the cockpit, often made of wood. No relation to what you do with your hair.

Gunwale (sounds like "tunnel"): the boat's rail at the edge of the deck.

Rub rail: a plastic, rubber, or wood rail placed around the boat to protect it in case you happen to come in contact with another boat or object.

Partners: a hole in the deck where the mast goes—not the people with whom you run a business.

Hydrofoils

Every sailboat has a centerboard, daggerboard, or keel, and a rudder. The main purpose of these various foils is to keep the boat from going sideways when sailing upwind. The rudder helps the boat turn. These hydrofoils are also carefully shaped to develop lift, which helps propel the boat forward.

Keel: a heavy appendage, often made of lead, fixed in place on the bottom of larger boats.

Centerboard: a thin board or plate located on the boat's centerline; it is raised and lowered by pivoting around a bolt or pin.

Daggerboard: a centerboard that slides up and down through the bottom of a hull, and is pushed in place with a stabbing motion.

Sideboard, Leeboard: pivoting boards that are located on the sides of a boat.

Rudder: the underwater blade at the stern of the boat, used for steering.

Tiller: a bar, usually wooden, connected to the rudder head and moved laterally by the skipper to steer the boat.

Hiking stick: an extension of the tiller enabling the skipper to steer from the windward rail.

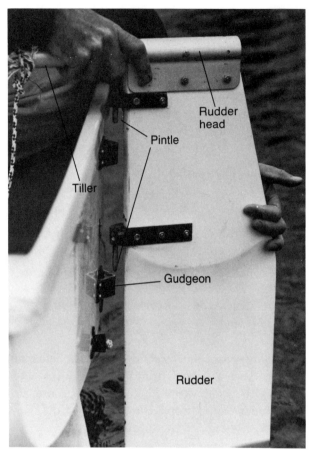

Tiller

Rudder head

Pintle

Gudgeon

Rudder

The rudder.
The rudder, located at the stern, is used for steering. It attaches to the boat with pintles that fit into gudgeons. The metal piece that extends forward from the rudder head is the tiller.

Gudgeon: a fitting, attached to the transom, that holds the rudder pintle.

Pintle: a metal fitting on the leading edge of the rudder; it fits into the gudgeon and allows the rudder to swing.

Most larger boats have keels to keep them from heeling (leaning) over too far. Cruising boats, which need to go in areas of shallow water, often use a combination keel/centerboard; the centerboard is lowered below the shallow keel for most efficient upwind sailing, but can be raised for shoal waters. We are also seeing more and more winged keels on cruising boats. Besides a marketing ploy resulting from the 1983 America's Cup race, these are an efficient way to give a boat more stability without a deeper keel (which would limit cruising ability in shallower waters).

Smaller boats that rely on the weight of the crew for stability have a centerboard or daggerboard, which can be raised and lowered. A centerboard pivots on a pin and is usually adjusted with a handle, block and tackle, or drum. Daggerboards, on the other hand, slide up and down a through-hull slot.

The rudder is the primary means of steering the boat and is also a carefully shaped foil. On most small boats, you steer with a tiller that is fastened to the top of the rudder. This can be permanently attached or may be removable, in which case it must be secured tightly while sailing. Many tillers have an extension called a hiking stick, which allows you to move your weight farther outboard while steering.

If your rudder is the removable type, insert it when the water is calm, preferably before you hoist the sails. The rudder is held in place by a combination of pintles and gudgeons that are very difficult to line up if the boat is bouncing around. Be sure to engage the safety catch to keep the rudder from popping out. Some rudders can pivot in the rudder head, which allows you to attach the rudder before you launch the boat. It also means that you will have to pull and secure the rudder downhaul line to keep the rudder in position.

Spars

Spars are the poles used to support the sails. The biggest spar is the *mast*. For centuries, masts were made of wood, but now most are aluminum extrusions. On some smaller boats, such as Lasers and Finns, the mast is free-standing and is supported only at its base. As masts get taller and need to hold up more sail area, however, they must be supported by wires called *stays*. The stays on the side of the mast are called *shrouds;* the *forestay* and *backstay* support the mast in fore and aft (front and back) directions.

The *boom* is a shorter spar that's connected to the mast with a swiveling device called the *gooseneck* (one of the more colorful sailing terms). The boom attaches to the bottom of the mainsail, allowing you to control the trim of the sail. It usually hangs at about head height, so you have to watch out while sailing or you'll get a "boom" on the head.

Another spar that we will discuss more thoroughly in Chapter 7 is the spinnaker pole, which also attaches to the mast and, as its name implies, helps support the balloon-shaped sail called the spinnaker.

Mast

Gooseneck

Boom

BUST #10

The swivel fitting that attaches the inboard end of the boom to the mast is called the gooseneck.

Rigging

The *standing rigging* refers to all the rigging that stands in place, including:

Shrouds: wires that hold up the mast from the side of the boat.

Spreaders: struts on the side of the mast that hold the shrouds out, increasing the sideways support.

Turnbuckles: threaded devices used to adjust the length of the shrouds.

Chain plates: eyes or straps on the hull to which the shrouds are attached.

Running rigging refers to all the rigging that "runs" (can be moved), including:

Halyards: lines (ropes) or wires used to hoist sails.

Sheets: lines used to pull sails in and out.

Guy: the spinnaker sheet, on the windward side of the boat, that goes through the spinnaker pole.

Outhaul: the line that attaches to the lower aft corner of the mainsail (the clew) and pulls the sail toward the end of the boom.

Cunningham: a line system at the forward end of the boom used to adjust the tension along the forward edge of the mainsail. It was named after a famous America's Cup sailor, Briggs Cunningham, who popularized its use.

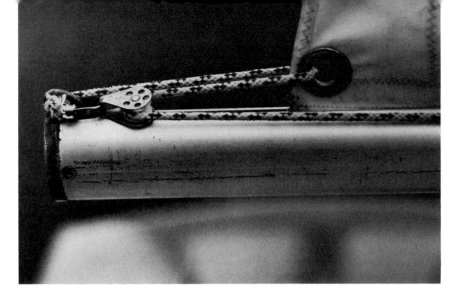

The outhaul is a line and purchase system used to pull the clew of the mainsail toward the aft end of the boom.

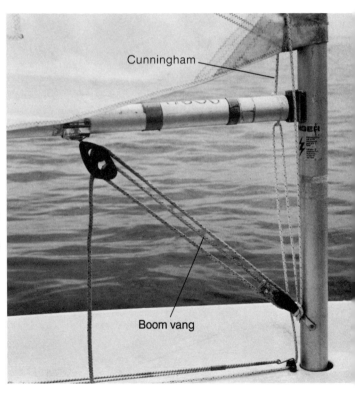

Cunningham

Boom vang

The boom vang is usually a block and tackle that runs from the boom to the bottom of the mast. Its purpose is to keep the boom from flying up into the air. The cunningham controls sail shape by adjusting tension along the luff.

Boom vang: block and tackle attached to the underside of the boom, about a third of the way back (aft) from the mast. The boom vang is used to hold the boom down in heavy air so you can maintain good sail shape and control.

Hardware

There are a lot of gadgets and doohickies on sailboats. In fact, boats are a tinkerer's delight—something you know if you have ever had to maintain one.

Cleat: a device used to hold line securely when under pressure. There are many types of cleats for different uses. Two of the most popular are the *cam cleat,* which has two jaws that pivot to hold the line between them, and the *clam cleat,* which has two jaws in a vertical plane.

Blocks: pulleys used for gaining mechanical advantage or simply for turning lines around corners. A *ratchet block* turns one way only so it's easier to hold a line under tension. A ratchet is most commonly used for the mainsheet.

Cam cleats and clam cleats.
A cam cleat has two pivoting jaws with teeth and a spring inside that hold a line in place.

A clam cleat is a stationary one-piece device with jaws to hold a line in place. To release the line, simply pull it out of the jaws.

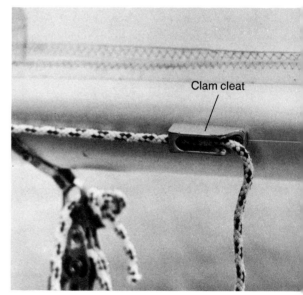

Cam cleat

Clam cleat

Sails

In the previous chapter we described how the wind makes a sailboat go. Now let's take a closer look at the sails that harness this energy.

Depending on the type of boat you sail, and the direction you are going relative to the wind, there may be one, two, or three sails in use at any one time. Some square-riggers carried 30 or more sails, with names like "mizzen upper topgallant" and "fore royal." At present, we are concerned with the three most common sails—the mainsail, the jib, and the spinnaker.

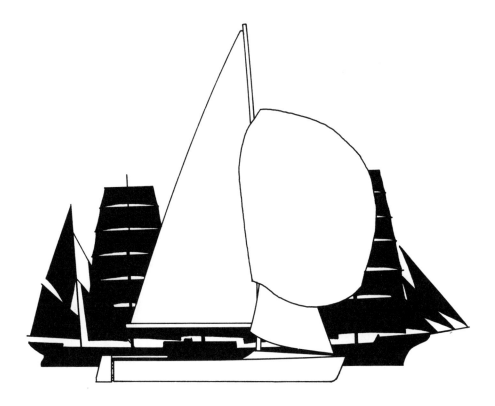

Sails.
Most modern small sailing boats are sloop-rigged with three sails—a far cry from the past, when it wasn't uncommon for sailboats to have several masts and as many as 30 sails.

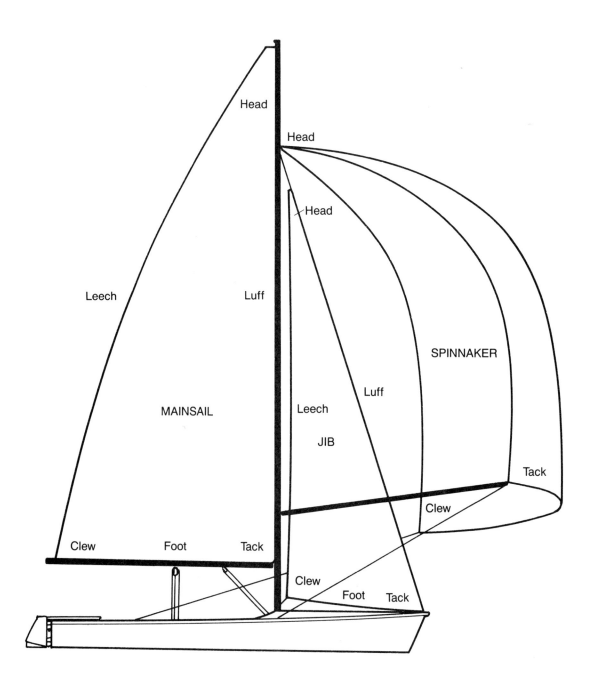

Sail parts.
The main, jib, and spinnaker each have three corners called the head, tack, and clew. The main and jib have three sides: the luff, leech, and foot.

The *mainsail,* as you might guess, is the primary sail on a sailboat. Every boat has one attached to the mast and boom. There are several different ways that a mainsail can be fastened to these spars, including slides that fit on a track, bolt rope that fits into a groove, or a sleeve that fits over the mast (as on a Laser). The mainsail can also be "loose-footed," attached to the boom only at the corners (the tack and clew).

A *jib* is a smaller sail in front of the mainsail, hoisted along the forestay. It is usually attached to the forestay with hanks or snaps. Sometimes the jib has its own internal wire that acts like the forestay when pulled tight. If the jib is large and has a significant overlap with the mainsail, it is called a *genoa.* Most small boats have jibs, while most larger boats (over 25 feet) use genoas.

Boats that have only a main and no jib are called *cat-rigged.* Some popular cat-rigged boats are the Laser, Finn, C Scow, and Hobie 14. Boats with a main and a jib (and only one mast) are called *sloops.* Almost all popular small sailboats today are cats or sloops.

The *spinnaker* is a very large, full sail that is used when the wind is coming from the side or back of the boat. It's usually very colorful and requires a bit of practice to get it flying right. (More on spinnakers in Chapter 7.)

Each of these three sails—the mainsail, jib, and spinnaker—has a unique function and appearance, but they all have certain things in common. Their three corners and three edges all have the same names:

Head: the top corner of the sail.

Tack: the lower forward corner of the sail.

Clew: the lower aft corner of the sail.

Luff: the forward edge of the sail.

Leech: the aft edge of the sail.

Foot: the bottom edge of the sail.

4

Getting Started

A sailboat on the water is a very different animal from the sturdy structure that sits on a trailer ashore. It tips, moves, and will steer itself unless you take control. Like many sports, sailing requires a good deal of technique. If you've ever watched an experienced sailor, you may agree it's a little like watching ballet. The boat carves precise turns, the sails remain full, and the sailor's body appears to be an extension of the boat. Learning the right technique—where to place your body, how to move in the boat, and how to steer—will make learning to sail a lot easier and safer.

RIGGING AND HOISTING THE SAILS

To put the mainsail on, first find the foot and clew of the sail. Slide the clew along the boom. At the end of the boom is the outhaul, which may be either a shackle or a piece of line. This attaches to the grommet in the clew and allows you to adjust the tightness of the foot of the mainsail. Next, attach the tack of the mainsail to the gooseneck; usually this is held with a pin.

Before hoisting the mainsail, there are three other controls with which you should be familiar. The *cunningham,* which is also called the *downhaul,* is used to tighten or loosen the luff of the sail once it is raised. The *boom vang* controls how tightly the end of the boom is pulled down, thus affecting the amount of tension on the leech. And the *mainsheet* is used to pull in or let out the sail. We'll explain how to adjust these controls to get the best performance out of your mainsail in Chapter 8.

When you're ready to put the jib on, begin with the tack. This attaches with a shackle, pin, or hook at the base of the forestay. If your jib has hanks

51

Sailing well requires a solid grasp of technique and an innate sense of "feel" for the boat's response to varying conditions.

Rigging the Mainsail

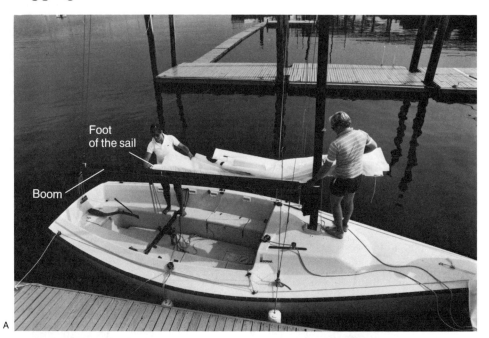

Foot of the sail

Boom

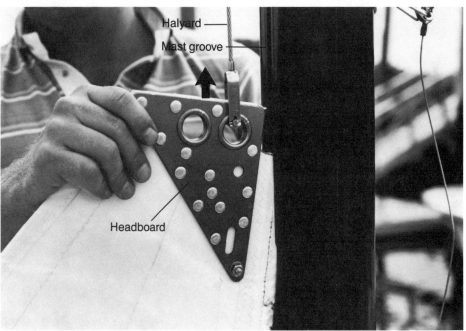

Halyard

Mast groove

Headboard

When putting the mainsail on the boat, the first step is to slide the foot of the sail along the boom (A). Then slide the headboard into the groove on the mast, and attach the halyard (B).

Rigging the Jib

To put the jib on, fasten the
hanks to the forestay, attach
the halyard to the head (A), and
fasten the jib tack to the base
of the forestay (B). Don't forget
to tie the jib sheets to the clew
(bowlines work best) (C).

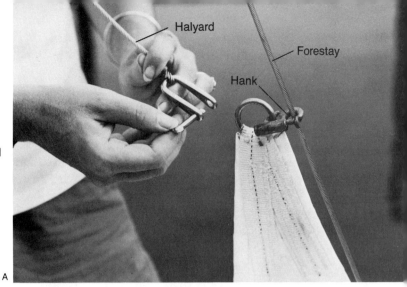

A

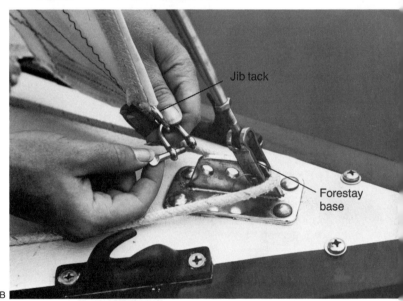

B

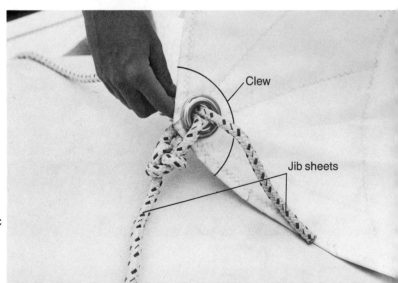

C

or snaps, fasten these around the headstay, starting with the one closest to the tack. Next, tie or snap the jib sheets into the grommet at the clew of the jib. One sheet is led back on either side of the mast, through the jib leads, and then tied with a figure-eight knot at each end. The jib sheets allow you to trim the sail in and out (more about jib trimming in Chapter 8).

You are now ready to hoist the sails. It's usually a good idea to raise the mainsail first. Attach the main halyard to the head of the mainsail, making sure the halyard leads straight from the top of the mast. Ease the mainsheet, boom vang, and the downhaul so they will not restrict you from raising the sail all the way to the top.

Next, position your boat so the bow is headed into the wind. This is very important. It means there will be less pressure on the sail, the halyard won't jump out of the sheave (turning block) at the top of the mast, and the head of the sail, or the battens, won't get caught inside the shrouds. You do not want the boat to start sailing away before you are ready to go.

It is easiest if two people raise the mainsail together. One person should pull up the halyard as the other feeds the luff of the sail into the mast. If you have trouble getting the sail all the way up, check to be sure that nothing is caught and that the control lines are released. If the weight of the boom makes raising the sail difficult, have someone hold up the end of the boom.

Hoisting the Main

When hoisting the mainsail, the first and most important step is to position the boat so that the bow is pointed into the wind (A).

Have one person hoist the halyard while a second crew member feeds the luff of the sail into the groove and a third crew member holds up the end of the boom (B).

Once the sail is all the way up and securely cleated, carefully coil the halyard so it can be quickly released in case of emergency. In a recent J/24 championship, the fleet was approaching the finish line when a squall hit, with 50-knot gusts. The smartest boats were able to drop their sails immediately, while those who couldn't sustained a lot of damage to their sails.

Once the main is up, you are ready to hoist the jib. Attach the jib halyard to the head of the jib, again making sure that the halyard is clear. Then pull up the sail. Raising the jib is usually a lot easier than hoisting the main. (The spinnaker is used only when sailing downwind. We'll describe how to attach and raise it in Chapter 7.)

SAFETY EQUIPMENT

One of the most important parts of sailing is ensuring the safety of your boat and crew. This means thoroughly checking to make sure that all the boat's equipment is in good working order and that you have all the required safety gear. In addition, as mentioned earlier, you should always be aware of the weather conditions.

Make sure the mainsheet, boom vang, and cunningham are eased completely (C).

When the mainsail has been raised all the way to the top of the mast, cleat the halyard snugly (D).

Many sailboats use a ball-and-slot arrangement to cleat the halyard to the mainmast, or a loop-and-hook arrangement, as shown here (E).

Safety

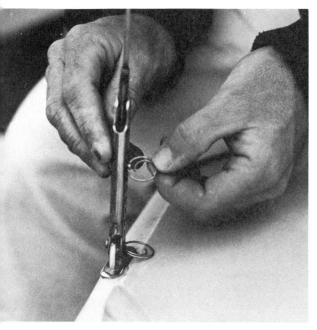

Each day before going sailing, you should perform a safety check. Among other things, be sure to look at all the pins that keep the mast in place.

Before going out, also make sure the flotation tanks are dry. Then screw the port covers securely in place so they won't leak in case of capsize.

Before going sailing, you should routinely check for wear and tear on the parts of your boat—especially those that are constantly under stress, such as the rudder pintles and gudgeons, hiking straps, and rigging. Check all the pins and shackles to be sure that the pins are securely in place. Wrap tape over the pins so they cannot come out, and also so they don't expose a sharp edge that might tear sails, clothing, or skin.

If your boat has air tanks for flotation purposes, the port covers or plugs must be snugly in position to keep the tanks airtight. Any water that gets into these tanks should be removed, and if there is a leak, it should be sealed, as these tanks keep the boat floating if it capsizes or fills with water. Some boats have through-hull bailers that drain water when the boat is moving fast; make sure these are shut tightly when you launch your boat and first set off.

It's essential to carry the proper safety gear. The Coast Guard requires specific equipment to be carried on various-sized boats, and some states have additional regulations. Check with your local Coast Guard Auxiliary to ensure that your boat is properly equipped. You *must* have one personal flotation device on board for each person, as well as a throwable cushion or life ring if your boat is over 16 feet long. It's critical that the flotation device be the proper size as well, since one that is rated for a 60-pound child is not suitable for a 200-pound adult. We'll talk about safety in detail in Chapter 11.

POSITION IN THE BOAT

Where to stand or sit in a sailboat is not always clear to the beginning sailor. Sometimes it's even tricky for advanced sailors. We remember a 420 regatta at Yale University a few years ago. When one of the top sailors got onto his boat, he stepped onto the bow. Unfortunately, his weight caused the boat to heel way over; as he grabbed the mast for balance, he succeeded in tipping the boat over on top of him as he fell backward into the water. It was a shocking (and embarrassing) way to relearn the fact that you have to be very careful where you put your weight on small boats!

The safest way to get on a centerboard boat is to step into it from the side while someone else is holding it steady. Once you're on board, put the centerboard (or daggerboard) all the way down. The weight and the lateral area of the board in the water will help steady the boat. As you move around the boat, you'll notice that the closer you stay to the mast and centerboard, the less the boat tips. The farther you go toward the gunwales (sides) or the bow and stern, the more your weight makes the boat tip.

When you actually sit down in the boat to start sailing, there are a number of things to consider when positioning yourself. Most of these depend on whether you are the skipper or the crew.

Skipper

The *skipper,* or helmsperson, is the person who holds the tiller and keeps the boat from crashing into other boats. The skipper's sitting position must allow him or her to hold the tiller or hiking stick comfortably, trim the mainsheet, and see the sails, wind, and water. To do all these things, the skipper usually sits on the windward rail, just forward of the end of the tiller and even with the mainsheet block. This is a good spot for several reasons:

Visibility. Sailors have known for a long time that the higher you are off the water, the more you can see. That's why the explorers and whalers sent crew members up into "crow's nests." On any boat, the higher you sit, the better you can see the wind and waves on the water. Therefore the helmsperson should

The skipper's sitting position.
The skipper, or helmsperson, must be able to hold the hiking stick, trim the mainsail, and see the sails, wind direction, and water—all at the same time. The best place to sit and do all this: on the windward rail.

try to sit on the windward rail most of the time, since this is the highest—and usually the most comfortable—position. Sitting fairly far forward will also give the helmsperson a good view of the telltales on the jib and the water in front of the boat.

Mobility. The skipper must be able to cross easily from side to side during tacks and jibes. Therefore you should sit near the space between the end of the tiller and the mainsheet block, since you must cross between these.

Ease of trimming. As we'll discuss later, the skipper usually trims the mainsheet while steering. Therefore he or she must sit close to the mainsheet block so it's easy to cleat, uncleat, and adjust the mainsheet.

Weight. The location of your weight will also affect boat speed. In general, the skipper (and crew) should move forward in a light breeze, to keep the stern from dragging, and aft in strong wind and waves, to keep the bow from plowing.

Crew

While the skipper stays mostly in one spot, the rest of the crew must be a lot more flexible. Crew priorities include balancing the heel of the boat, trimming

The crew's sitting position.
The crew should sit just forward of the skipper. Besides being cozy, this keeps the live weight centered in the boat.

the jib, and helping the skipper look around. The best place for the crew is usually just forward of the skipper, within easy reach of the jib cleat. You also must be able to move easily from side to side. Considerations include the following:

Weight: Sitting just forward of the skipper allows total weight (crew and skipper) to be centered fore and aft, which reduces the boat's pitching and keeps the stern from dragging or the bow from plowing. It's also a lot cozier.

Maneuverability: With the skipper sitting on the windward rail, the crew must move his or her weight to windward or leeward to keep the boat from tipping too far in one direction. If you're not hiking on the windward rail (more on hiking later), face forward with one foot on each side of the centerboard trunk so you can move either way quickly.

Visibility: It's the crew's job to keep a lookout for wind puffs, waves, and other boats, especially in places where the skipper has a blind spot. These include the area to leeward that is obscured by the jib, and everything behind the skipper's back.

Ease of trimming: The crew must be ready to trim or tack the jib at any time, so he or she should be within reach of both starboard and port jib sheets.

WHAT TO HOLD

Now that you have some idea of where to put your body, what about your hands? Who holds what, and why?

Skipper

The skipper normally controls the tiller with the aft hand and the mainsheet with the forward hand. While this means he has his hands pretty full, holding just one would be like driving a car and letting someone else press the accelerator. It feels strange, and it's hard to coordinate the two. As we'll explain later, the mainsail and helm are closely related, so it's best to have the same person control both.

Most small sailing boats have tillers with hiking sticks. Our preference is to steer as much as possible with the hiking stick and avoid holding on to the tiller directly. Reason: The hiking stick lets you sit outboard and forward. There are only a few times when we'd suggest steering directly with the tiller: when the air is so light that the skipper has to sit inside the boat (to help heel the boat to leeward), and when you're sailing downwind in breezy conditions on the edge of control.

There are at least three different ways to hold on to the hiking stick: (1) "underhand"—holding the hiking stick on your aft side with your fingers wrapped around it; (2) "overhand"—holding the stick across your lap with your fingers wrapped around it; and (3) "pencil grip"—holding the hiking stick like a pencil, with the end pointed toward your chest. Our preference is the latter, though you should certainly use what's most comfortable for you. The advantage of the second and third styles is that your aft hand is near your mainsheet hand and can therefore help when trimming the main.

As skipper, you should hold the mainsheet in your forward hand. You can grip the sheet by simply wrapping your hand around the line, or when there is a lot of pressure on the sheet, you can wrap the sheet around your hand. If you do this, be sure you can quickly release the sheet in case you get a puff.

There are a number of ways to make trimming the main easier. Most boats have cleats built into the base of the mainsheet block, which make it easy to cleat off the main once it's trimmed properly. However, we don't ever recommend cleating the mainsheet, for two reasons: first, since the wind and the boat's course are always changing, you have to adjust the mainsheet constantly to keep the sail working properly; second, in order to prevent a capsize when you get a puff, you have to be able to ease the sheet immediately to spill the excess wind. This is difficult if the sheet is cleated.

Holding the Hiking Stick and the Mainsheet

The skipper usually holds the hiking stick in his aft hand and the mainsheet in his forward hand.

Hold the hiking stick with any grip that is comfortable. Options include: underhand . . .

overhand . . .

. . . and the pencil grip.

Holding the Mainsheet

Hold the mainsheet firmly in the palm of the forward hand.

For a better grip, wrap the sheet around your hand, but be sure you can release it quickly.

When the wind is blowing, it's a good idea to wear sailing gloves. This allows you to hold the sheet without cleating it, which is better for safety and sail trim.

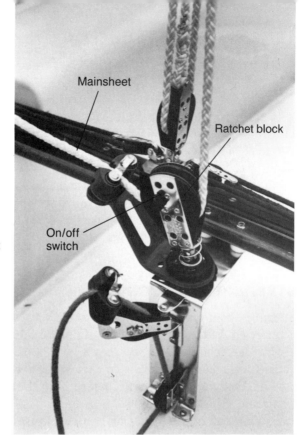

Mainsheet

Ratchet block

On/off switch

A ratchet block turns in one direction only and therefore makes trimming the mainsail much easier on windy days. In light air you can turn the ratchet off to let the block spin freely in both directions.

A ratchet block provides a nice compromise between holding the sheet and cleating it. This block is made to turn in one direction only. It lets you pull the sheet in, and then locks so the line won't slip out. However, it releases as soon as you let go of the sheet. The locking system can be turned off on light-air days so the sheet can run freely in both directions.

Another way to make trimming the mainsail easier is by using as much purchase in the sheeting system as possible. On some boats, you can increase the number of parts in the mainsheet to get better mechanical advantage. We generally prefer, however, to use as few parts as possible (usually a two-to-one advantage), since this gives the best feel for the sail and also allows us to ease and trim the sail quickly. However, it's often a good idea to use three or four parts, especially on bigger boats or in heavy air.

Finally, wear sailing gloves on windy days if you have tender hands (we'll talk more about gloves in Chapter 11). And when you sheet in, hike out at the same time so your entire body, not just your arms, will be helping trim the main.

Crew

As a crew, you're lucky because you have fewer things to hold than the skipper, at least when sailing upwind. Your primary responsibility is the jib sheet. It's o.k. to cleat the jib sheet, but it's a good idea to keep it in your hand, or at least within easy reach. When there's a chance you will tack or jibe, hold on to both jib sheets. On a windy day you can use the jib sheet to help support your weight while hiking upwind. Downwind you will be very busy with the spinnaker (if your boat has one)—something we'll talk more about in Chapter 7.

STEERING AND TURNING

Steering a boat may seem like one of the simplest things about sailing, but it's actually an art that requires a lot of practice. Just getting used to a tiller takes a while, especially if you've spent a lot of time driving a car. It's a little like going to England and having to drive on the left-hand side of the road. After a while, though, it will feel normal to push the tiller left when you want to go right, and vice versa.

While the rudder is normally used to turn a boat, other variables such as weight placement and sail trim can have just as great an effect on where the boat goes. In fact, with a little practice you could even leave the rudder at the dock and still have a nice sail. However, the best way to control the boat is to use a combination of rudder, crew weight, and sail trim.

The Rudder

If you've ever been in a rowboat or canoe and stuck one oar in the water, you know the boat will turn toward that side. A rudder works along similar lines: It directs the stern of the boat in one direction and turns the boat by pivoting it around the centerboard or keel. It's important to keep a few principles in mind when you are steering with the rudder:

• You can't steer if you are not moving. The rudder will work only when water is flowing over its surface. A common mistake beginning sailors make is to jam the rudder over and try to turn the boat when they're not going anywhere. You have to build speed before you can turn.

• Steering with the rudder slows you down. The farther you push the tiller to one side, the more of the rudder's surface area will be exposed to the flowing

The rudder is your primary means of turning and steering. Every time you turn the rudder, however, it acts as a brake, as you can see by the turbulence in this photo. Therefore, don't steer more than necessary.

water, and the more the rudder will act as a brake. Oversteering is like slamming on your brakes to do a skid turn rather than gently guiding your car around a curve.

• Steering with the rudder is more effective when your centerboard or daggerboard is all the way down. In fact, if your board is all the way up, the boat will go sideways when you turn the rudder.

Sail Trim

You can use your sails like the rudder, to turn the boat around its underwater pivot point. Sailboards are a great example of how this works. Since boards don't have rudders, they have to rely on the position of the sail for turning. If you have ever watched a board sailor, you've noticed that when she wants to turn away from the wind (or "bear off"), she'll push the whole sail forward over the bow. There is now more wind pressure pushing on the bow, so the board will pivot around the centerboard (the underwater pivot point).

The same principle applies to a sailboat. If you want to turn away from the wind, pull the jib in tight and let the main way out. This moves the effective sail area quite far forward, which pushes the bow away from the wind. If you want to head up toward the wind, let the jib luff and trim the main in tight. Now the working sail area is behind the centerboard, so the boat will turn toward the wind.

Using Sail Trim
to Steer the Boat

WIND

The boat has now started
turning away from the wind (D).

To make the boat turn the other
way, the crew trims the jib in
tight. This pushes the bow away
from the wind (C).

As the boat turns toward the
wind, the skipper eases the
mainsheet out to slow the rate
of turn (B).

The crew of this Snipe has
removed the rudder to show
how you can use sail trim to
turn the boat. To make the bow
head up toward the wind, the
skipper (left) is trimming the
mainsheet (A).

By trimming the jib tight and easing the main, the boat will stop turning toward the wind and will begin to head off again. It's amazing how much of a snake course you can make without a rudder (G)!

The combination of trimming the main and easing the jib has started the boat turning toward the wind again (F).

To make the boat head up toward the wind again, the crew eases out the jib while the skipper trims the main (E).

Weight Placement

Another factor that determines how a boat will turn is the shape of its bottom. When a boat is level (not heeled to windward or leeward), the part that is in the water is shaped symmetrically—exactly the same on both sides. This makes the boat want to continue forward in a straight line. However, when you heel the boat one way or the other, the underwater shape changes and is no longer symmetrical. The result is that the boat will want to turn.

If you know how this works, you can shift your weight to help steer the boat. For example, if you want to turn to port, make the boat heel over to starboard. When you do this, the underwater hull shape on the starboard side becomes much more curved than on the port side, and the boat will turn to port to follow that curve. The opposite is true if you heel the boat to port: it will tend to turn to starboard.

To understand how these three steering forces work together, try a few exercises (once you are fairly proficient at sailing). First, sail along on a close reach (more on "reaching" in a moment) and try to head off without changing the position of your weight or letting out the sails. This will be difficult if it's windy. Then repeat the same exercise—only this time ease your mainsail and hike out so you heel the boat slightly to windward. It should be a lot easier to turn the boat.

When you're ready, try sailing without your rudder (a medium breeze is best). Steer by moving your weight from side to side; then steer only by trimming and easing the mainsail and jib. If you are successful at this, you will have gained a great deal of mastery over your boat. (One word of caution: Before taking your rudder out, be sure you will have a calm spot where you can put it back in.)

Heeling

One of the factors that causes a boat to turn is the degree to which it is heeled. When a boat heels to port, for example, it will tend to turn to starboard.

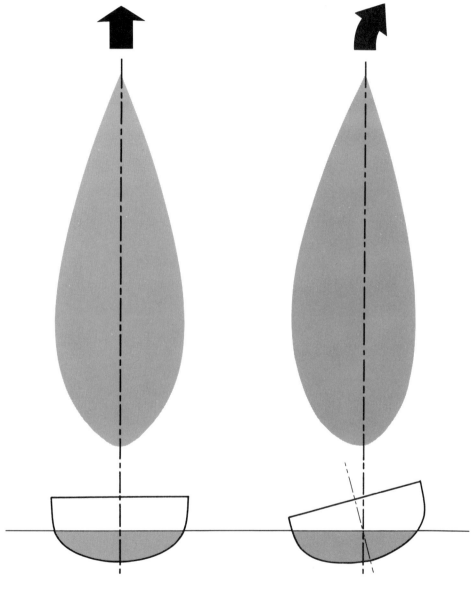

When the boat is level, the underwater portion of the hull is symmetrical, and the boat will tend to sail in a straight line.

When the boat heels to port, the underwater portion of the hull becomes asymmetrical. The greater curvature on the port side will make the boat turn to starboard.

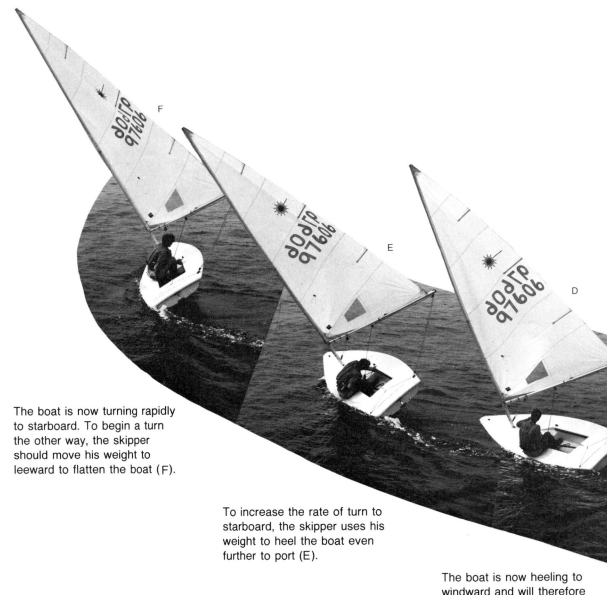

The boat is now turning rapidly to starboard. To begin a turn the other way, the skipper should move his weight to leeward to flatten the boat (F).

To increase the rate of turn to starboard, the skipper uses his weight to heel the boat even further to port (E).

The boat is now heeling to windward and will therefore start turning to leeward (D).

The boat is now turning rapidly to port. To begin a turn the other way, the skipper starts leaning outboard (C).

C

B

To make the boat turn to port (toward the wind), the skipper leans in to heel the boat to starboard (to leeward) (B).

A

The rudder has been removed from this Laser to demonstrate how crew weight can be used to steer the boat. During this example, the mainsheet stays cleated (A).

POINTS OF SAIL

Now that you know how to turn it, let's talk a little about where you will point the boat. The most common way to explain the course sailed by a sailboat is to describe the angle between the boat's heading and the direction of the wind. This is called the *angle of sail.* It's easiest to picture this by imagining a huge compass rose, with the wind coming from due north and your boat in the middle. Let's look at what happens as the boat turns clockwise around the points of the compass.

When the boat is heading due north, it is sitting *head to wind,* and its sails are luffing (flapping loosely). No boat can sail straight into the wind; if it stays in this position very long it will lose headway. At that point you'll have trouble turning the boat, and you are said to be "in irons," a term that dates back to square-rigger days. We'll talk more about this in the next chapter.

The closest a boat can sail to the wind is around 40 or 45 degrees. This means that the boat in our example will have to turn toward the northeast (or northwest) in order to fill her sails. On this course her sails will be trimmed in all the way, and we'd say she is sailing "close-hauled" or that she is "beating" to windward. A boat steering northeast will be on port tack because her boom is on the starboard side of the boat.

As our boat heads farther away from the wind, we say she is "bearing off." Between northeast and east, she is on a *close reach* with her sails eased slightly from the close-hauled position. When the boat heads east, she is *beam reaching,* since the wind is now coming from abeam (at a right angle to the boat). She is still on port tack.

As our boat continues to bear off, her crew eases the sails farther out. When she heads southeast, she's on a *broad reach,* and when she steers due south her sails are out as far as they can go. This position is called "running," or going dead downwind. Notice that with the wind dead astern, the mainsail boom could be on either side. If it remains on the starboard side, then our boat stays on port tack. But if a crew member pulls the boom over to the other side, then the boat has jibed and she is on starboard tack.

To complete the circle, our boat heads up toward the wind on starboard tack, passing again through broad reaching, beam reaching, and close reaching. When she gets to northwest, she is steering close-hauled on starboard tack; if she steers any closer to the wind, her sails will begin to luff and she'll lose speed. In order to head northeast again, she has to tack—swing her bow through the wind. Her sails will luff and cross the centerline of the boat, putting her on port tack once more.

Points of Sail

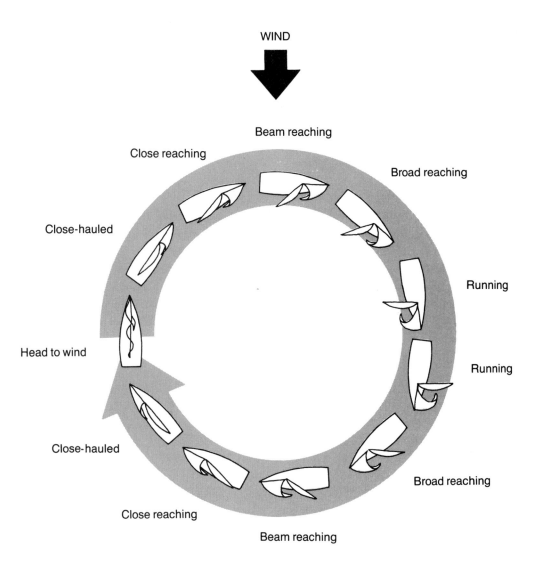

A boat's "point of sail" depends on the angle between her centerline and the wind direction.

Polar Diagram

WIND

Knots of boat speed are measured on both the vertical and horizontal axes, and are shown by concentric circles as well.

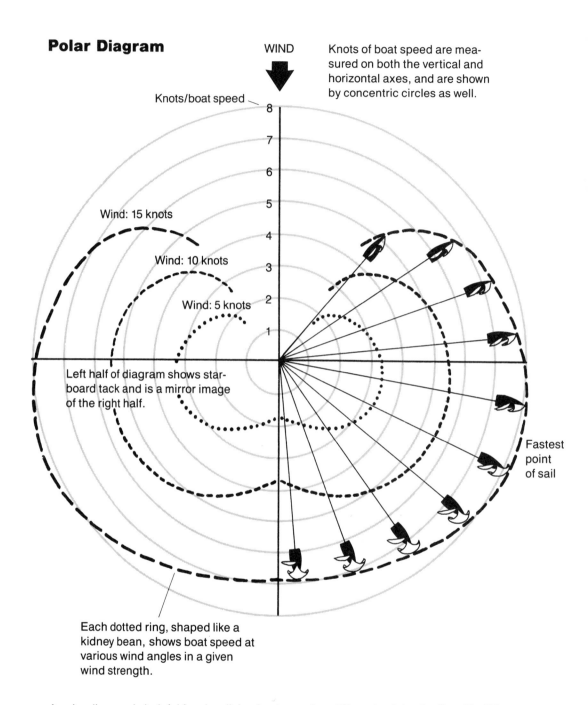

Knots/boat speed

Wind: 15 knots

Wind: 10 knots

Wind: 5 knots

Left half of diagram shows starboard tack and is a mirror image of the right half.

Fastest point of sail

Each dotted ring, shaped like a kidney bean, shows boat speed at various wind angles in a given wind strength.

A polar diagram is helpful for visualizing boat speed on different points of sail and in different wind velocities. First, the harder the wind blows, the faster the boat goes. Second, the fastest point of sail occurs with a true wind angle of about 110 degrees. And third, the slowest points of sail are straight upwind and straight downwind.

Polar Diagram

The speed of a sailboat varies according to her angle of sail. A boat on a beam reach, for example, will sail significantly faster than a boat that is close-hauled or running.

An interesting way to visualize the differences in speed is by using a graph called a polar diagram. This shows how fast a boat will go at every point of sail. It also shows that increases in wind velocity will generally make a boat go faster.

5

Sailing Upwind

As we mentioned in the last chapter, no boat can sail straight into the wind. It's a nice idea, but unfortunately it doesn't fit too well with the laws of nature. Successfully sailing upwind is a little like driving up a mountain. You can't go straight up, so you have to follow a winding course, zigzagging back and forth.

In a sailboat, the hairpin turns are called *tacks*. To reach an upwind destination, you have to sail as close to the wind as you can, tacking back and forth between close-hauled courses on starboard and port tacks. This is one of the greatest challenges in sailing. It is also one of the most artistic. There's nothing like taking the helm on a windy day and settling into an upwind "groove" where the boat almost sails itself to windward.

How close you can point to the wind depends on your boat, as well as on wind and sea conditions. The typical square-rigger, for example, could sail only about 65 degrees to the wind. This meant that from close-hauled on starboard tack to close-hauled on port tack was an angle of 130 degrees. As you might guess, it took these boats a long time to make progress upwind; that's why they sailed routes in the "trade winds," where the breeze was behind them most of the way.

It wasn't until the development of sails oriented fore and aft (instead of athwartships as with the square-riggers) that boats improved their upwind performance significantly. One of the reasons the English armada defeated the Spanish in the 16th century was their superior upwind ability. This enabled the English to establish and maintain positions to windward of the larger Spanish ships, which gave them a huge fighting advantage.

Today's sailboats can sail upwind better than any in history. With more efficient keel and hull shapes, it's not uncommon for modern keelboats like Solings or Etchells-22s to sail 35 degrees to the wind. When 12-Meters sailed

77

Making a boat sail into the wind is one of sailing's biggest challenges. Yet, when you find the upwind "groove," it is also one of the most rewarding.

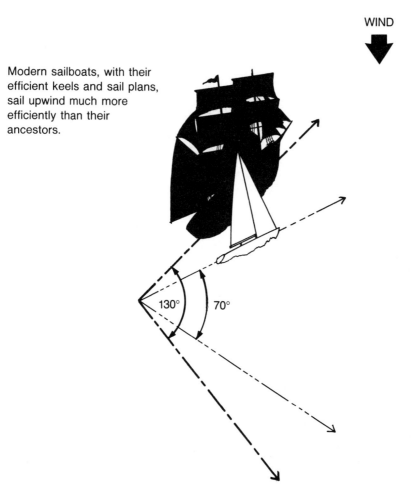

WIND

Modern sailboats, with their efficient keels and sail plans, sail upwind much more efficiently than their ancestors.

130°   70°

for the America's Cup in the heavy winds off Perth, Australia, it was typical for them to sail a true wind angle as small as 32 degrees (or a tacking angle of only 64 degrees!). The tacking angle is narrowest when seas are smooth and winds are strong.

STEERING UPWIND

When your destination is to windward, you have to sail close-hauled, continually trying to point your boat as close to the wind as possible. This takes a bit of practice, because you can't just aim the boat for a buoy or a distant point on shore the way you can at other times. And there is no magic dial to tell you when you are sailing close-hauled. There are, however, a few guidelines.

Preparation. Before you begin sailing upwind, sit on the windward rail with the hiking stick in one hand and the mainsheet in the other. Have your crew hold on to the jib sheet. Now feel the wind on your body. Use the wind ripples, telltales, and masthead fly to get a rough idea of the wind direction. Turn the boat so you are heading perpendicular to the wind (beam reaching).

Sail trim. Now start trimming in both the mainsail and the jib so your boat accelerates. As soon as you have some speed, start heading closer and closer to the wind. Each time you head up, trim your sails in a little tighter so they stop luffing. When you reach a close-hauled course (about 45 degrees to the wind), your sails should be trimmed in tightly. (We'll talk a lot more about sail trim in Chapter 8.)

Where to look. The skipper should concentrate on the front part of the jib, along the luff of the sail. If you're on a boat without a jib, such as a Laser, watch the front part of the mainsail. You are looking for two things: (1) a bubble, or backwinding, along the front of the sail; and (2) movement of the windward and leeward telltales on the sail.

Steering by the sail. Many people learn to sail upwind by using the front part of the jib (or the main on a catboat) as a guide. This is a good basic technique. With the sails trimmed in tight, keep trying to steer a little closer to the wind. When the front part of the jib just starts to backwind (or luff), you are sailing as close to the wind as possible.

Steering by the Sail

The best way to keep your boat sailing efficiently upwind is to watch the front of your jib or, as shown here, your main when you don't have a jib. When the front of the sail just starts to luff, you are sailing as close to the wind as possible.

WIND

If you head up any farther, more of the wind will hit the back of the jib and a larger part of the sail will luff. This is called *pinching.* If you continue sailing this close to the wind, you'll feel the boat start to slow down. When you want to make distance to windward, continually try to point the boat as high as possible without pinching and slowing down too much.

Steering by the telltales. Another good way to know how high (close to the

Steering by the Telltales

Another good guide for sailing upwind is the telltales near the front of the jib (right). By watching the relative action of the windward and leeward telltales, you will know how close you are sailing to the wind.

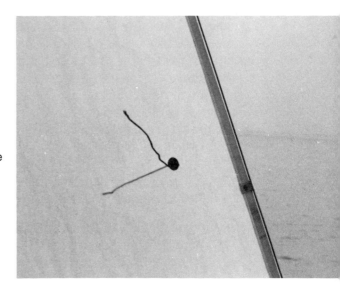

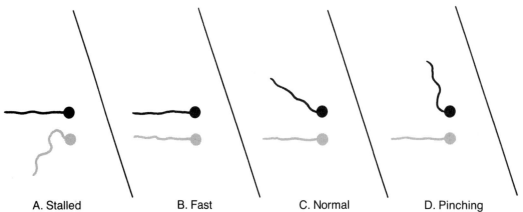

A. Stalled   B. Fast   C. Normal   D. Pinching

When the leeward telltales on your jib (the lighter ones shown here) are dancing around (A), it means the airflow behind the jib is stalled. You should head up more toward the wind. When the windward (darker) telltales are lifting straight up (D), you are pinching. This is fine in heavy air, but in light air you will be going too slowly. It's more common to sail upwind with the telltales somewhere between these two extremes (B or C).

wind) you can point is by watching the telltales on the jib (or the main on a catboat). These pieces of yarn are usually taped onto the sail about a foot back from the luff. Start out by sailing close-hauled, with the telltales on each side of the sail streaming straight back. Then head up slightly. When the jib is about to luff, the windward telltales will start to lift up above a horizontal position. This is a good upwind heading. If the windward telltales get more active than this and start to spin around, you are pinching too much.

Telltales will also indicate when you are not sailing as high as possible. If the leeward telltales start to flutter or drop out of a horizontal position, then you are sailing too low and losing distance to windward. In this case, head up until the leeward telltales straighten out and the windward telltales just begin to move again.

Practicing. Finding the upwind groove is a matter of practice as much as anything. You have to spend time sailing close-hauled, watching the luff of the jib and telltales, and constantly trying to head a little higher without losing speed. If you have a chance to sail upwind next to another boat, you'll get a quick and accurate idea of how efficient a job you're doing. Ultimately, if you can close your eyes and keep your boat going upwind, you'll know you really have the "feel."

Sailing upwind requires a good feel for the boat. One way to develop this feel is to try sailing with your eyes closed. Just make sure your crew is keeping a good lookout!

TACKING

Steering a boat on a close-hauled course is only part of the challenge of getting to an upwind destination. You can sail close-hauled all day, but if you remain on one tack, you are only zigging and not zagging. Making progress upwind requires sailing on both tacks.

The act of tacking, by definition, takes you from one tack (starboard or port) to the other, with your bow swinging through the wind. The sails begin to luff as you push the tiller over, they flap wildly when you are head to wind, and then they fill again as you reach a close-hauled course on the new tack. Before you begin a tack, consider the following requirements:

1. *Boat speed.* First and foremost, your boat has to be moving before you can tack. If there is no water flowing over the rudder, the boat won't turn when you push the tiller over. So don't try to tack when you're going slowly. Instead, turn the boat away from the wind to fill the sails and pick up speed. Then tack when the boat's momentum is sufficient to carry her around through the turn.

2. *Angle of sail.* A boat normally tacks from one close-hauled course to another. If you begin a tack from a reaching course with the sails halfway out, it can be difficult to spin the boat all the way through the wind without losing speed. So before you tack, trim your sails in to the center of the boat and head up to a close-hauled course.

3. *Room to maneuver.* Tacking involves an abrupt (90-degree) turn that may not always be anticipated by other boats. So before you push the tiller over, look around to make sure you have room to tack. Remember that while you are tacking, you must stay clear of other boats.

Tacking Mechanics

Once you've got good speed on a close-hauled course, and have plenty of room on all sides, you are ready to tack. Here is the step-by-step procedure—everything the skipper and crew should do before and during this maneuver.

First of all, the skipper should tell the crew about upcoming tacks. Not all crews are good mind readers. A friend of ours had to make an unexpected tack in one race at a recent Thistle National Championships. He had to avoid another boat and unfortunately didn't have time to warn his crew. When he came out of the tack, his crew was still in the hiking straps—underwater on the leeward side. The moral is, if your crew is not ready, a tack can result in disaster.

To make sure everyone is ready, the skipper typically yells, "Ready about?" at least a few seconds before the proposed tack. What the skipper is saying is: "I'm about to throw the helm over. Are you ready to let go of the old jib sheet, trim in the new, and move to the other side?" When the crew is prepared, they should respond, "Ready." This is a signal for the skipper to begin the tack.

When we are racing, we modify this procedure slightly. We tell our crew that when we say "Ready about," we'll assume they are ready to tack unless we hear an objection. This usually works, but in a less pressured situation we'd suggest waiting for a positive response.

Executing the tack itself is a skill that takes a little practice. The skipper's first move is to push the tiller to leeward, slowly at first and then faster as the boat reaches head to wind. While this is happening, the skipper, facing forward, stands up, moves across the cockpit, and turns so he can sit on the new windward rail. He exchanges the mainsheet and tiller behind his back just before he sits down, and then he brings the tiller back to centerline as the sails fill on the new tack.

The crew's job is usually a little easier. When the skipper says "Ready about," take the jib sheet out of the cleat and hold it. Then grab the windward sheet and pull all the slack out of it. Just before the boat reaches head to wind (and the whole jib begins luffing), release the old sheet (making sure it runs freely) and trim the new sheet. While you're doing all this, you must move across the cockpit to the other side.

Roll Tacks

Just as with any maneuver, tacking is more effective if you use your weight and the sails to help steer the boat. In racing, the aggressive use of crew weight during a tack is called *roll tacking*. This technique works best for lightweight boats in light and medium winds.

To roll tack, heel the boat a little farther to leeward as you go into the tack. As we explained earlier, this helps the bow round up into the wind. When the boat reaches head to wind, roll it sharply to windward by hiking out hard on the rail. Just when your backside is about to get wet, cross over to the new windward side and hike out to flatten the boat again. You've now performed a state-of-the-art racing tack.

Tacking

As the skipper continues turning the boat, the starboard crew member trims in new jib sheet. The port-side crew member makes sure the old jib sheet runs out freely (D).

D

When the jib begins to luff, the crew member on the port side releases the jib sheet (C).

C

The skipper, who has the mainsheet in one hand, begins the actual tack by pushing the tiller to leeward (B).

B

A

F

Once the sails are filled, the crew relaxes and continues to sail upwind. Nice job! (F)

E

The skipper, turning so he faces forward, moves to the new windward side. He exchanges the mainsheet and hiking stick from one hand to the other, behind his back (E).

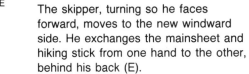

The first step in executing a tack is for the skipper to yell "Ready about!" At that signal, the crew grab each of the jib sheets and respond, "Ready!" (A)

The Roll Tack

A roll tack works best in small, lightweight boats when there is not too much wind.

C

As the former windward rail hits the water, the skipper and crew move quickly across the boat with sheets in hand (C, D).

B

Just before the boat gets head to wind, the skipper and crew hike out hard to "roll" the boat over to windward (B).

A

A roll tack begins like any other, with the skipper pushing the tiller to leeward and the boat heading up into the wind (A).

Boat
direction

D

E

Both crew members turn, facing forward, and trim the sails as they sit on the new windward rail to flatten the boat (E). The sails are eased slightly to accelerate on the new tack.

F

Once the boat is up to speed, the sails are trimmed to gain maximum efficiency (F).

In Irons

One of the pitfalls of tacking is the possibility of getting caught "in irons." This usually happens when your boat is going slowly to begin with, or when it hits some waves as the tack begins. The result is that the boat ends up pointing directly into the wind and stops moving forward. With the sails luffing and the boat starting to move backward, this can be a tough situation.

The best way to deal with being in irons is to avoid it in the first place. First, don't try to tack unless you have a good amount of boat speed. Second, avoid tacking from reach to reach. Trim your sails in tight and always begin your tack from a close-hauled course. Third, if the seas are rough, turn the boat quickly through the wind so the waves won't kill the boat's momentum before you're on the new tack.

In irons.

When you are stuck in irons (pointing into the wind), there are two ways to escape. First, you can push the boom out to "back" the main (left). Or you can hold the clew of the jib out to back the jib (right). Once the boat starts backing up, push the tiller toward the boom (away from the jib). It's as easy as backing out of a parking spot!

If you do get caught in irons, keep calm. It will give you a good opportunity for some boat-handling practice. The best idea is to encourage the boat's natural inclination to drift backward. What you want to do is to get the boat moving through the water so you can use the rudder to turn the bow away from the wind. Hold your main boom out to one side (this is called *backing the main*), and push the tiller toward the boom. If you do this right, the boat will turn as if you were backing out of a parking spot.

Another way to get your bow pointed away from the wind is to back the jib: the crew grabs the jib's clew and holds it out so the jib fills on one side. At the same time, the skipper pushes the tiller to the opposite side. It's the proven principle of using your sails to help steer.

HEELING

One thing that scares many beginning sailors about going upwind is heeling, or leaning to one side. Boats tend to heel more when sailing upwind because the sails are angled so that the wind's force hits them sideways. Centerboard boats are tippy and heel quite a bit since they don't have much ballast to counteract the force on the sails. However, it's also easy to flatten them by hiking out (leaning out over the windward side).

Keelboats won't respond as much to crew weight, but they usually have a good deal of lead in their keels, so they won't tip so easily. Because of this, they offer a very steady ride. And you'll be secure knowing it's almost impossible to capsize a boat with a keel.

When a boat does heel, it can be either scary or fun, depending on your state of mind. In very light air, it's good to make the boat heel a little so the sails will sag to leeward and keep their shape. As the wind gets heavier, however, it's better for performance and for peace of mind to sail the boat as flat as possible. There are several reasons to minimize heel in breezy conditions:

1. If you heel too far, the boat will capsize and you'll get wet. This isn't too much fun unless it's a hot day and you're in a boat that can easily be righted, like a Sunfish or Laser.

2. The farther you heel, the more you sideslip, because your centerboard or keel no longer extends down so far into the water. The famous winged keel on the 1983 America's Cup winner, *Australia II,* was designed with this in mind. When the boat heeled, the leeward wing actually stuck down farther into the water.

Heeling.
Once you've learned to control the boat and are no longer afraid of capsizing, heeling becomes a natural part of sailing upwind.

3. As you heel more and more, the rudder starts coming out of the water and becomes less effective, which makes steering more difficult.

4. Finally, heeling to leeward makes the boat want to head up toward the wind. This tendency is called *windward helm,* because your helm (rudder) is trying to make the boat turn to windward. To counter this force, you have to keep pulling the tiller to windward, which means more work for you and slower boat speed because the rudder is dragging more.

In windy conditions, sailboats have a tendency to heel more than you might want them to. When this happens, the skipper and crew have to work together to keep the boat flatter. The first thing to do is to get your weight as far to windward as possible. On most small boats, this means sitting on the windward rail and hiking out. For us, this is one of the most thrilling parts of sailing.

Many boats have hiking straps along the centerboard trunk; you hook your feet under them and lean way out to windward. While you're hiking, hold on to the main or jib sheet to support some of your weight. The farther you lean out, the better leverage you will have with your weight and the less your boat will heel.

Some boats use trapezes to get crew weight out even farther. With a trapeze, the crew (and sometimes the skipper as well) wears a harness with a

Hiking

Hiking is fundamental to sailing
a small boat upwind in a
breeze. To keep the boat flat,
hook your toes under the straps
and lean back as far as you
dare.

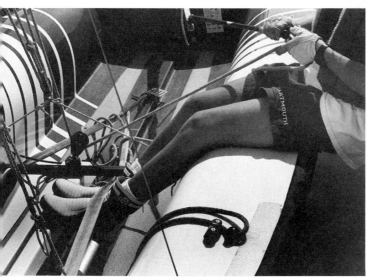

Hiking straps provide a leverage
point for leaning backward.

For maximum hiking, some
boats are equipped with
trapezes.

WIND

Pinching.
One way to keep a boat flat when it's windy is to "pinch," or steer the boat toward the wind so the front part of the jib begins to luff. This takes some of the wind pressure out of the sails, causing the boat to heel less.

built-in hook. This hook is connected to a wire that runs up to the mast, allowing the crew to put his or her feet on the rail and actually stand off the side of the boat, parallel to the surface of the water. Trapezing is an exciting, and wet, part of sailing.

Simply moving crew weight to windward will not always keep your boat flat. When it's quite windy, you must use other methods to control heeling:

• *Pinch:* When you start to heel too much, simply push the tiller to leeward a little so the boat heads up and the front part of the jib luffs. On a very windy day, it's not uncommon to sail upwind with 25 percent of the jib luffing to keep from heeling too much.

• *Ease the sails:* Heeling is caused by wind pressure on the sails, so if you want to stop heeling, simply let your sails luff. Be sure to hold the mainsheet on windy days, and let it out whenever a puff makes you heel too much.

• *Depower your sails:* When it's windy, a flat sail shape will cause less heeling than a full sail. The technique of making your sails less powerful is a bit advanced, so we will explain more in Chapter 8.

The best way to make heeling less scary is to make sure you and your crew are well versed with capsize procedure, just in case. And anyone who is not a proficient swimmer should always wear a life jacket. (More about safety in Chapter 11.)

UPWIND "FEEL"

As we said at the beginning of this chapter, sailing a boat upwind requires experience and a sensitivity to the way your helm feels. You will surely know it when the boat settles into the "groove." Things just feel right, and the boat almost sails itself.

It's possible to know a lot about sail trim, weight distribution, and boat performance by tuning in to the feel of your hiking stick.

Windward (or weather) helm: Windward helm is the tendency for a boat to turn toward the wind when you let go of the tiller. It's good to have a little windward helm when sailing upwind, because this gives you a positive feel and helps the boat track to windward. Too much helm, however, means you will have to pull too hard on the tiller to keep the boat going straight. Reduce this helm by flattening the boat.

Windward Helm

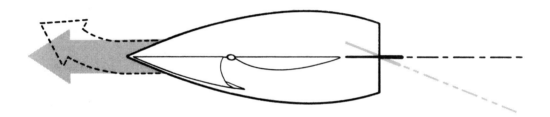

Most boats will turn toward the wind if you let go of the rudder. This tendency is called "windward helm." It's good to have a little windward helm to give the boat a lively "feel." But with a lot of helm, which happens in heavy air, you will have to turn the rudder quite a bit to keep the boat going straight. This slows you down and stresses the rudder as well.

Neutral helm: With neutral helm, your boat will keep going straight when you release the tiller. This is ideal for downwind sailing, but it provides a mushy feel upwind.

Leeward helm: When you let go of the tiller, a boat with leeward helm will turn away from the wind. This is common in light air, but it's never desirable. You can get rid of leeward helm by making your boat heel more and trimming the sails in a bit.

Every crew member should try to feel how the boat is going. This is much easier for the skipper, of course, because he or she is connected to the hull and the water through the tiller. That's why I suggest giving everyone on the boat a turn at steering. Besides, steering offers a great way to learn and have fun.

6

Sailing Downwind

Upwind sailing requires a bit of precision. You have to keep the sails and the boat on edge in order to make your way to windward. When you turn downwind, however, you can really cut loose!

Sails are eased as the boat heads off and the wind and waves send you off on what can be one of the most exhilarating rides of your life. Your local amusement park has nothing as thrilling as planing across the water and surfing down the face of a big wave. Or as relaxing as being lazily pushed along by a breeze on a sunny day.

"Downwind" sailing is a broad and inclusive term. Generally, any point of sail not close-hauled is considered to be downwind. You remember from Chapter 4 that this includes close reaching, beam reaching, broad reaching, and running. Reaching is going in a direction across the wind, while running is truly going with the wind.

A general rule of thumb in sailing downwind is that the more you head off away from the wind, the more you let your sails out. On a run, your sails should be eased as far as possible so their maximum area is exposed to the wind. Notable exceptions to this are catamarans and iceboats, which encounter much less friction than traditional boats. When these boats bear off onto a reach, they accelerate quickly and build up their apparent wind. This makes them go even faster, which further increases their apparent wind and moves it forward.

Even though the true wind is coming from behind, these catamarans and iceboats move so quickly that it feels as if the wind is coming from the bow. Therefore their sails must be trimmed in tightly. Like any boat, however, an iceboat begins to slow down when it heads too far away from the wind. This is because the apparent wind and true wind begin to work against each other, which reduces the apparent wind.

97

Running downwind can be one of sailing's more exhilarating experiences.

Unlike upwind sailing, you can head anywhere you want when going downwind. Two easy ways of maintaining a steady course are steering for a point on land or holding a constant compass heading.

One of the major differences between upwind and downwind sailing involves how you steer the boat and trim your sails. Going upwind, you generally pull the sails all the way in and then use them as a guide to steer the boat. When sailing downwind, however, you usually aim the boat straight for where you want to go, and then use this heading as a guide for trimming your sails.

One of the easiest ways to steer downwind is to aim for an object such as a buoy or a point on shore. Be sure it is fixed, though. We once heard a story about a sailor on an overnight race who was steering for what he thought was a light on shore. After a while, the crew discovered they were way off course. It turned out the helmsman had been following a slow-moving barge!

A more accurate means of steering is by compass. Aim your boat in the direction you want to go and note the compass heading. Then hold this course on the compass. In that race, the helmsman could have known that his "fixed" object was moving if he had been watching the compass.

Another way to determine a compass course is to use a navigational chart. In fact, this is the only way to do it when you can't see your destination. One thing we don't like about using a compass is that you get mesmerized by numbers. We'd much rather look around at the water and the sky.

Once you're steering the downwind course you want, you must trim your sails accordingly. Ease the sails out as far as they will go until they just begin to luff along the forward edge; then trim them in slightly.

Since it is very difficult to steer a perfectly straight course, and the wind is usually shifting in direction and/or velocity, you must constantly adjust the sails in order to keep your boat performing optimally. Keep the sheets in your hands so you can trim or ease when necessary. Telltales on the shrouds, or a wind pennant on the top of the mast, will let you know the apparent wind direction and can tip you off to any changes that would require an adjustment in sail trim.

Other good sail trim guides are the telltales at the forward part (luff) of your sails. You can use the flow of these telltales to determine how far to ease your sheets. For example, if the windward telltales are dancing (moving around), the sail is probably luffing slightly and should be trimmed. If the leeward telltales are dancing, the air flow around the sail has stalled, and the sail needs to be eased. Ideally, both telltales should flow straight back (or the windward telltales should be lifting slightly). In Chapter 8 we'll discuss techniques for getting optimum downwind performance out of your sails.

Trimming your sails.
When sailing on a reach, the skipper eases the mainsheet until the front of the sail just starts to luff (or the windward telltales start dancing). Then she trims the sheet back in just a bit. Getting the most out of your boat is a constant process of easing the sail as far as possible without luffing.

Centerboard

Upwind, the centerboard keeps the boat from going sideways. Downwind, however, the centerboard creates drag, so it should be raised to reduce wetted surface. Pull it up halfway on a beam reach and almost all the way on a run. Also, keep your weight forward in light air and gradually move aft as the wind increases.

There are several other things you should consider when sailing downwind:

Centerboard. Upwind, the centerboard (or daggerboard) keeps the boat from going sideways and develops lift, which helps the boat move forward. As you head downwind, however, the board is much less critical because you are heading more in the direction that the wind is trying to push you. Therefore you can gradually raise the centerboard as you head off away from the wind. This reduces the drag caused by pushing the board through the water, allowing you to sail faster.

In general, you want to raise the centerboard just a bit on a tight (close) reach, one-third of the way up on a beam reach, one-half on a broad reach, and three-quarters on a run. If your boat gets tippy, however, lower the board a bit for increased lateral stability. Be sure to lower the centerboard all the way before you turn back upwind.

Weight placement. The ideal fore-and-aft positions of the skipper and crew vary according to wind and wave conditions. In light air, move your weight forward to keep the stern from dragging in the water (which slows you down). As the water gets choppier, move back far enough to keep the bow from plowing into waves.

You also want to move aft as the wind increases. This will give you more stability because the aft sections of most hulls are flatter and therefore less tippy than the forward sections. When it's windy enough so the boat will lift up and

The goal downwind is to have a "neutral helm"—that is, if you let go of the rudder, the boat should keep going straight. This is usually accomplished by sailing the boat flat on its lines. When the wind is directly behind, however, a little heel to windward is often the fastest way to go.

WIND

"plane" on the water surface, move your weight even farther toward the stern.

Your athwartships weight placement should also vary with the conditions. When sailing downwind, you want to have the helm balanced so the boat is steering straight. This minimizes drag on the rudder. It is best to let the skipper sit in a comfortable position and then have the crew move so the boat has a neutral, or balanced, helm. (The helm is said to be neutral when you can let go of the tiller and the boat continues in a straight line.) Then by leaning in or out slightly, the skipper can steer the boat and at the same time feel the helm changes in the tiller. In general, it's good to keep the boat flat when going downwind.

When you have a windy beam reach, all crew weight will need to be hiking out on the windward side. On a broad reach, the crew may be to leeward and the skipper to windward. When on a run, you may even have to heel the boat a bit to windward to achieve a balanced helm. Athwartships weight placement also affects the boat's lateral stability. That is, the closer your weight is grouped near the centerline of the boat, the easier it is for the boat to roll. So spread as far outboard as possible whenever you need stability.

Spinnaker. This large, full, colorful sail can improve your speed on a beam reach, broad reach, or run. Setting a spinnaker is fun, but it requires a bit of practice, so we've covered this in much more detail in Chapter 7.

Sailing by-the-lee. Pretend you are sailing on a run with the wind coming directly over your transom (stern). Now head off even farther so the wind is coming over your leeward stern quarter. This is called sailing "by-the-lee." It can be dangerous because the wind may fill on the back side of the mainsail and cause an unexpected jibe, sending the boom flying across the boat with extreme force. This has not only caused many headaches, but has even killed some sailors on larger boats over the years.

There are several ways to tell when you are sailing by-the-lee: (1) You'll feel the wind coming from the leeward side (and you'll see it coming from this direction on the telltales and/or masthead fly); (2) the leech (aft edge) on your mainsail will start to flop back and forth; and (3) there will be very little pressure on your mainsheet. If you find yourself by-the-lee, head the boat up toward the wind (by pushing the tiller toward the boom) or jibe. Be sure to watch out for your head.

Wing and wing. When you are sailing on a very broad reach or a run and you don't have a spinnaker, you can gain speed by "winging" your jib or genoa to the windward side. When the jib starts to lose its wind because it is behind the mainsail, try pulling it over to the windward side to catch the wind. This is called sailing "wing and wing."

Sailing wing and wing.
When the wind is coming from behind, you can gain speed by sailing "wing and wing." Pull the jib over to the windward side of the boat and hold the jib sheet outboard (away from the main) so the sail will fill (left). Some boats, such as the Star and Snipe (shown here), have a whisker pole (right) for holding the jib in the wing and wing position.

WIND

Whisker pole

On smaller boats, you can usually use your arm to hold the jib sheet out far enough to windward to fill the sail. But on bigger boats, you'll need something longer to hold the jib out far enough. Try using your spinnaker pole or a specially designed whisker pole (standard on racing boats like the Snipe or Star). Attach the end of the pole to the clew of your jib or genoa, and attach the other end of the pole to the mast. Then use the windward jib sheet to trim the sail.

You'll find there is a relatively small apparent wind angle where a winged jib will work effectively. If you head off too far, you'll go by the lee. If you head up too far, the leech of the jib will fold back on itself. But when you can make winging work, your boat will fly.

HEELING

When it's windy, your boat can heel going downwind as well as upwind. Close and beam reaching are the times when you are most likely to be overpowered, because then the wind is blowing directly across your boat. There are several ways to control heel downwind. The most exhilarating of these is to use all of your body weight as leverage by hiking out to windward. Sometimes this will be enough to keep the boat flat.

If you are already hiking and the boat is still heeling too much (you're "overpowered"), ease the sails so they luff slightly. This spills some of the wind and depowers the boat. Even though you are wasting wind power, the most important thing is to keep the boat flat. In puffy conditions, be sure to keep the mainsheet in your hand so you can ease the sail quickly whenever you get a puff.

There is one other good way to stop a boat from heeling. As you remember from Chapter 5, you can flatten a boat upwind by heading up toward the wind (called pinching or feathering). When you're going downwind, the best way to reduce heeling is to head *away* from the wind. This lessens the sideways forces on the boat. Note that this is the exact opposite of sailing upwind.

Sometimes, when you are on a breezy run, your boat will start to roll back and forth until it seems a little out of control. There are several ways to minimize this. One is to put the skipper and crew on opposite sides of the boat and use your weight to counter the rolling. At the same time, steer in the direction of the rolls: when the boat heels to windward, head up; when it heels to leeward, head off. This will keep the boat under the sails as much as possible.

Another way to prevent rolling is to overtrim your sails slightly and put more tension on the boom vang. You can also head up onto more of a broad reach. All of these methods should steady the boat.

Broaching.
If you lose control because a gust of wind hits while sailing on a reach, the boat will heel over and head up toward the wind. This is called broaching. To prevent it, keep the boat flat by easing the sails out and heading off (away from the wind).

JIBING

Jibing (or gybing) is to downwind sailing what tacking is to upwind. Like tacking, jibing takes you from one tack to the other; but it is the stern, rather than the bow, that passes through the wind. The sails go from one side to the other, but since they are eased out for a broad reach or a run, they come across very quickly and with a great deal of force as the wind fills on their back side.

The reason to jibe is usually that the other tack provides a faster course to your destination. Or it may simply be that the other tack offers more sunshine. In racing, you often have to jibe around a buoy as part of the course. Some boats, like iceboats and catamarans, or most boats in very light wind, go very slowly when they sail on a dead run. In order to get downwind they jibe back and forth, maintaining their speed from reach to reach. This is called "tacking downwind"—it's a lot like the zigzagging you have to do to get to an upwind destination.

Before you jibe, check the position of the centerboard. It should be lowered most of the way to help stabilize the boat during the jibe. However, a contradiction occurs in windy conditions, when you might think that lowering the centerboard all the way would provide more stability. In fact, the boat can "trip" over the extended board and cause a capsize. In this case, keep the board up about one-third of the way.

Begin your jibe by heading off away from the wind. The skipper should grab the mainsheet between the ratchet block and the boom. Right at the moment when you feel the pressure in the mainsail soften, pull the sail in quickly toward the center of the boat; then let it go across the boat as the wind fills on the other side. In light air you can easily pull the sail across at any time; in heavy wind, however, you may need your crew to help throw the boom over.

The steering during a medium-to-heavy-wind jibe is crucial. When the sail comes flying across, all the force of the wind is now trying to push the boat over to the new leeward side. This effect is compounded by the centrifugal force of the turn, and the result is often a capsize. To avoid this fate you must steer an "S" course.

Begin the "S" by making your usual turn into the jibe. Just as the boom crosses the boat, turn slightly the other way so the boat is now aiming back under the sails. This keeps the boat from heeling too much right after the jibe. (Make sure the boom is crossing before you steer the other way, or the boom may not come across.) Once you are stable on the new jibe, head up to whatever course you choose.

During a jibe, the skipper crosses the boat while facing forward, exchanging the mainsheet and hiking stick behind his or her back. The crew also faces forward and is responsible for getting the jib onto the new tack as well as making any gross weight adjustments needed to keep the boat level. Since jibing is one of the most likely times for a capsize, it is smart to avoid jibing in heavy air until you gain more experience. In puffy winds, time your jibe so it takes place in a lull. If you are planing or surfing, however, the opposite is true. It is best to jibe when the boat is going as fast as possible so there is less pressure on the sails. This way they will come across more easily.

Jibing

A jibe happens when the boat
goes from one tack to the other
with the stern passing through
the wind.

Be sure to duck as the sail
crosses the boat, or you will get
a "boom" on the head (F).

Just when the wind starts to
catch on the back side of the
main, pull hard on the
mainsheet to bring the sail
across the boat (E).

As you turn the boat downwind,
grab the mainsheet where you
can easily give it a strong tug
(C, D).

Begin your jibe by turning the
boat away from the wind. Be
sure the centerboard is down
most of the way (A, B).

As the boom reaches the new
leeward side, ease the
mainsheet quickly to let the sail
out, and move your weight to
the new windward side (G, H).

Finish the jibe by exchanging the
hiking stick and mainsheet from
hand to hand behind your back
(I).

Steering an "S" course when jibing.

When it's windy, we suggest avoiding a jibe until you are proficient at sail-handling. If you do jibe, steer an "S" course—that is, begin your normal turn for a jibe, but as soon as the boom starts across the boat, steer back the other way a little. This keeps the boat under the sails and prevents a capsize to leeward on the new jibe. As soon as the boat is steady, you can steer the desired course.

PLANING AND SURFING

For many people, planing and surfing are the most fun parts of sailing. Only lighter-displacement boats with relatively flat hulls will plane, but you can get most boats to surf.

Planing occurs when a boat is going fast enough to lift up out of her own bow wave and skim across the water. If you think there's enough wind to get on a plane, bear off onto a beam or broad reach. Move your weight aft and hike out so the boat is flat, with a balanced helm. If the boat doesn't take off on its own, try a few quick and vigorous pumps on the mainsheet.

Surfing is just like riding a surfboard; instead of paddling with your arms to catch a wave, however, you use your sails and weight to catch a ride. The idea is to ride down the face of the waves like a surfer. Head up toward the wind to build speed, and when you see a wave trough right in front of your bow, bear off into it. Once you get on the wave, ride it for all it's worth. If you start

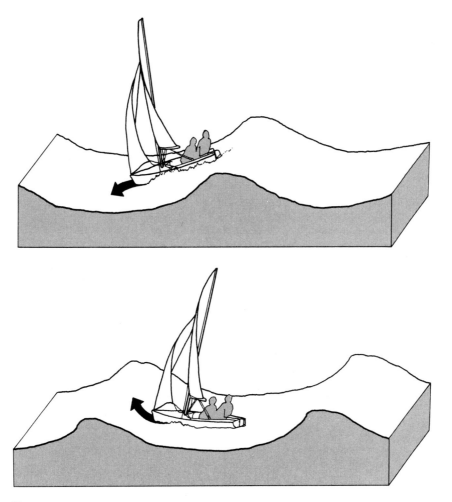

Surfing.
Surfing in a sailboat is a lot like catching the waves on a surfboard. When the wave is at your stern, bear off so you go straight down the face of the wave. As you approach the wave ahead, however, head up so you won't dig your bow into it. Then start looking for the next wave.

catching up to the next wave, turn slightly so you avoid plowing into it. When you start to slow down and feel as if you'll lose the ride, head back up and accelerate again.

Pumping and ooching will often help break your boat onto a plane or surf. (Besides that, they're fun and good exercise!) *Pumping* is rapid trimming and releasing of a sail. It effectively increases the apparent wind on the sail during the pump and can give you the burst of speed necessary to plane or catch a wave. *Ooching* is sudden forward and aft body movement and is very effective in initiating a surf. Just as your boat is starting to go down a wave, ooch forward sharply. At the same time give the sail a sharp pump or two (I like to grab the

Pumping

Pumping the mainsail is one way to help get your boat up on a plane or to surf a wave. The best way to pump is to grab the mainsheet straight from the boom (A), trim rapidly (B), then ease the sheet out as you accelerate (C).

A

B

C

mainsheet straight from the boom to make pulling easier), and off you go. In racing there are rules that limit when and how often you can pump or ooch, but when you're not racing, you can pump and ooch to your heart's content.

When you first plane or surf, the extra speed may seem a bit scary. You should remember, however, that the faster a boat goes, the more stable it is. So enjoy yourself and your newfound speed. When you get a puff, remember to bear off under the sails and keep the boat flat. This will get you onto an even faster plane. To stop planing or surfing, slowly head up and luff your sails until your boat speed drops. Put the centerboard down, trim in the sails, and you are ready to go back upwind.

One of sailing's greatest thrills is being on a small boat that's planing in a good stiff breeze.

7

Spinnakers

If you enjoy sailing downwind with just main and jib, wait until you set the spinnaker. It'll add a whole new dimension to your sailing. Imagine beating upwind for several miles on a breezy summer day, and then turning downwind. You hoist the spinnaker, trim the sheets—and *pop!* The colorful sail fills with wind, the boat lunges forward, and off you go, hopping over the waves, leaving the spray well astern. Now you're having fun.

Unlike the main and jib, the spinnaker (also called a "chute" or "kite") is designed specifically for reaching and running. Its shape is very full and round in order to catch a lot of wind. For this reason, a spinnaker cannot be flown when you're going upwind; as a general rule, you must be sailing at least 90 degrees to the true wind before hoisting.

Another difference between spinnakers and other sails is in the material. Almost all chutes are made of nylon, as opposed to the Dacron that's used for mains and jibs. Nylon is a stretchy, lightweight material that offers good tear resistance, easy handling, and the ability to fly well even in light air. Another advantage of nylon is that it comes in many colors, which means that spinnakers add visual excitement to an otherwise all-white world of sails.

The parts of a spinnaker have names very similar to those used for other sails. They differ, however, in one important way: With a main and jib, the tack stays attached at the center of the boat, while the clew changes from side to side. A spinnaker, on the other hand, is symmetrical.

The tricky thing about spinnaker terminology is that some parts have two names, depending on whether they're on the windward or leeward side. The clew that's attached to the spinnaker pole is actually considered to be the spinnaker's tack. The leech on that side is actually the luff. When the boat jibes, the pole is moved to the other side. That clew is then the tack, and that leech

113

Jibing a spinnaker in heavy air is one of sailing's more
challenging experiences.

becomes the luff. Fortunately, the head and foot of the spinnaker remain constant.

A *spinnaker pole* is always set on the windward side (the side opposite the boom) to hold the spinnaker out and away from the backwind of the main. One end of the pole is attached to the spinnaker pole ring on the forward side of the mast, while the other end attaches to the spinnaker sheet (called a *guy*). The height of the pole's outer end is controlled by the *topping lift*. Bigger boats also have a *foreguy,* which restricts the upward movement of the pole. Smaller boats use a *twing* line or a *guy hook* to hold the guy at the deck near the shrouds and eliminate the need for a foreguy.

Parts of a Spinnaker

A spinnaker is symmetrical from side to side, so the names of some parts are reversed when the boat changes tacks.

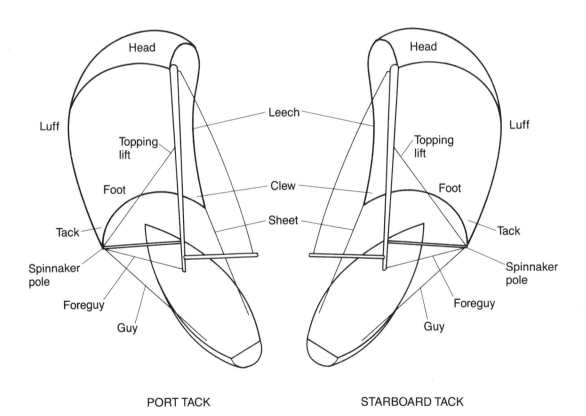

PORT TACK   STARBOARD TACK

The spinnaker pole helps the spinnaker to hold its shape and prevents it from collapsing. When sailing on larger boats, it's important to have a strong person on the pole.

Packing the Spinnaker

It's a good idea to pack your spinnaker into a "turtle" (in this case a basket) before leaving the dock. Lay the spinnaker out lengthwise with one clew on each side of the basket (A).

PACKING THE SPINNAKER

Before you hoist the spinnaker, you have to prepare it properly. It's like packing a parachute—if you're not careful, you'll end up with a tangled mess. Fortunately, the consequences of making a mistake are not quite so severe in a sailboat.

The best way to pack your spinnaker is by laying it out flat on a lawn or dock before you go sailing. Pull the head away from the foot, and follow both leeches from head to clew to be sure they are clear. Place a "turtle" (this can be a sailbag, bucket, or box) by the foot of the spinnaker and carefully flake (fold) the spinnaker into the turtle, beginning with the foot. I like to follow both leeches the whole way so I know they don't get twisted.

Leave both clews and the head hanging over the side of the turtle so they can easily be found when you need to attach the sheets and halyard. It helps if the corners are clearly labeled "Head" and "Clew" so you don't attach the halyard to the wrong corner. I can tell you from experience that raising your spinnaker sideways is one of the most embarrassing moments in sailing.

Once your spinnaker is in its turtle, you must decide whether to put it on the port or the starboard side of the boat. Figure out which side will be leeward when you sail downwind. This is where the spinnaker should be set up. Bring the ends of both spinnaker sheets and the spinnaker halyard around to the leeward side. Check to be sure they are not twisted and are led outside all other sheets and shrouds. There are three common ways to attach the spinnaker sheets and halyard: snap shackles, brummel hooks, and knots. Knots (preferably bowlines) are safest because they won't shake loose.

Making sure the leeches remain clear and straight, pack the entire spinnaker into the turtle (B).

When you are finished packing the spinnaker, it should be neatly stuffed into the turtle with the three corners of the sail sticking out (C).

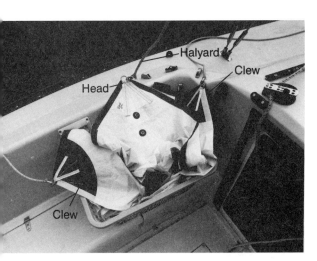

Once the spinnaker is packed, put the turtle on the port side of the boat (or on whichever side will be leeward when you set the spinnaker). Attach the spinnaker sheets to the clews and the halyard to the head (D).

The most common way to attach spinnaker sheets is with brummel hooks (shown here). However, we prefer to tie the sheets directly to the clews with bowlines, since these won't come undone.

THE SPINNAKER SET

Once you've packed the chute and attached the sheets and halyard, the only thing you have to do before hoisting is put up the spinnaker pole. Begin by resting the pole on the windward side of the foredeck. Put the windward spinnaker sheet (guy) into the forward spinnaker pole end fitting. Then attach the topping lift to the middle of the pole, and connect the aft end fitting to the ring on the mast. Tighten the topping lift and cleat it when the pole is roughly horizontal.

Putting Up the Spinnaker Pole

A   B

Before setting the spinnaker, the forward crew should put up the spinnaker pole. The first step in setting the pole is to hook the guy (the windward spinnaker sheet) into the forward end of the pole (A, B).

Close-up: attaching the spinnaker pole to the mast ring.

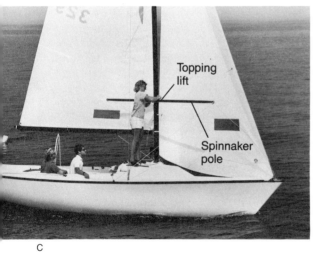

Topping lift

Spinnaker pole

C

D

Then push the pole forward and put the topping lift hook into the ring at the middle of the pole (C). Finally, push the pole all the way forward so you can attach the aft end of the pole to the ring on the mast (D). Adjust the topping lift so that the pole is roughly horizontal.

Setting the Spinnaker

Once the pole is up, you are ready to set the spinnaker. Head the boat off until you are sailing on a broad reach, and ease the main and jib sheets (A).

While the forward crew hoists the spinnaker halyard, the middle crew trims the spinnaker sheet and guy (B).

As the spinnaker is hoisted, the middle crew's most important job is pulling the guy so the spinnaker clew reaches the end of the pole. The forward crew helps by holding the pole forward to the headstay (here she has her hand on the foreguy to keep the pole forward).

You are now ready to hoist the spinnaker. If you have not already done so, head off onto your downwind course. One crew should begin hoisting the halyard, while another pulls the guy to bring the clew of the spinnaker around to the pole. In medium and heavy air, let the spinnaker sheet run free as you set so the sail doesn't fill before it is fully raised. As soon as the halyard and guy are cleated in position, trim the sheet to fill the spinnaker. And off you go.

One word of caution: If you are on a reach when the spinnaker fills, it will heel you over and make the boat head up. To counteract this force, head off as the spinnaker begins to fill, keep your weight on the windward rail, and be ready to ease your mainsheet. On most boats, the airflow to the spinnaker is disrupted by the jib, so the jib should be lowered as soon as the spinnaker halyard is cleated—especially in light or medium wind.

When the spinnaker is fully hoisted, the forward crew cleats the halyard. The middle crew starts trimming the spinnaker sheet to fill the sail (D).

As soon as the forward crew cleats the spinnaker halyard, she uncleats the jib halyard to drop the jib (E).

The forward crew pulls the jib down (F).

With the jib lowered, the spinnaker fills quite easily, even in this light air (G).

TRIMMING THE SPINNAKER

The three main controls for the spinnaker are the guy, the sheet, and the topping lift. The guy controls the fore and aft position of the spinnaker pole. When you first set the spinnaker, the guy should be trimmed so the pole is roughly perpendicular to the true wind direction, and it should be adjusted to maintain this angle as the wind changes.

On a beam reach, ease the guy so the pole (and tack of the spinnaker) is just to windward of the forestay. As you head off to a broad reach, gradually "square" the pole by pulling on the guy to bring the pole and spinnaker aft. On a run, the pole is squared all the way back against the shrouds so it's nearly perpendicular to the centerline of the boat.

Trimming the Spinnaker

Trimming the spinnaker sheet is an art that requires a bit of experience. Your goal is to ease the sheet as far as possible until the luff of the sail begins to curl. If the sheet is trimmed too tightly (left), the spinnaker will stall and pull you more sideways than forward. If you ease the sheet too much (right), the luff of the spinnaker curls a lot and the entire sail may collapse. The best trim setting is to have a very small curl (middle). That way, you will know the spinnaker is eased as far as possible without risking a collapse.

The spinnaker sheet, like the sheets on the main and jib, is used to trim the sail. Whoever trims the spinnaker should watch the luff of the sail. When the sail begins to "curl" (fold back over itself), trim the sheet until the sail is completely full again. Your goal is to keep the luff of the spinnaker constantly on the verge of curling. Any other trim will cause the boat to slow down or to heel excessively. Because the wind, waves, and heading of the boat are always changing (at least slightly), the spinnaker sheet must constantly be adjusted to get the most out of the spinnaker.

You can fine-tune the shape of the spinnaker by lowering or raising the pole with the topping lift. In general, you want to adjust the topping lift so the tack and clew are at the same height. In this position, the forward edge of the spinnaker should curl evenly up and down the luff.

Small curl

Adjusting the Spinnaker Pole

One of the biggest influences on spinnaker trim is the height of the spinnaker pole. Most spinnakers are designed to fly with their clews at even heights off the water (left). If the pole is too high (middle) or too low (right), it makes the clews uneven and distorts the smooth shape of the spinnaker.

JIBING

Jibing the spinnaker takes every available hand and can be tricky, especially in heavy wind. If you do it right, however, it can give you a great sense of accomplishment. The role of each crew member varies according to the size of your boat. Let's look first at a jibe with three crew members.

Three-Person Jibe

As you begin to head off to jibe, the sheet trimmer pulls the spinnaker guy aft (squaring the pole) and eases the spinnaker sheet so the sail stays square to the wind. At the same time the skipper, who is steering the boat through the jibe, eases the mainsail. The forward crew releases the twing on the guy (or takes the guy out of the guy hook) just before the jibe, and pulls the twing tight on the sheet. He or she then steps up on deck (or reaches the pole from the cockpit on smaller boats) and prepares to "jibe" the pole.

During the jibe, the skipper continues to turn the boat (steering an "S"

Pole too high.   Pole too low.

course in heavy air, as we discussed in Chapter 6) and pulls the main across. The trimmer, who is facing forward with one spinnaker sheet in each hand, flies the spinnaker so it stays full during the jibe. The forward crew unclips the pole from the mast and attaches this end to the sheet (which will become the new guy). At this point the pole is attached to both sheets. The pole is then detached from the old guy (using the trip line on the spinnaker pole to open the jaw), and this end is then clipped onto the ring on the mast.

In a good jibe, the spinnaker will never collapse. However, this takes a lot of practice. Whenever it's windy, it may take a bit of effort to push the pole out on the new windward side so you can attach it to the mast. We suggest bracing your back against the mast to get extra leverage. Once the jibe is complete, the forward crew steps back into the boat and helps balance, checking to see if the sheet trimmer needs a hand getting the new guy into the cleat.

On a boat with more than three crew, the basic jobs are the same, but the responsibilities are spread out. A fourth crew, for example, might adjust the twings during the jibe or help with one of the spinnaker sheets.

Jibing the Spinnaker

Jibing the spinnaker can be a real challenge, especially when it's windy. (For purposes of demonstration, the mainsail, normally up during a jibe, has been removed here.)

On a three-person boat, the forward crew handles the pole, the middle crew trims the spinnaker sheets, and the skipper steers and handles the main (A).

The first step is for the forward crew to take the pole off the ring on the mast. While she is doing this, the middle crew must adjust the sheets to keep the spinnaker square to the wind (B).

The end of the spinnaker pole that was on the mast now goes on the spinnaker sheet (which becomes the guy) (C).

Try to keep the pole horizontal during the jibe so it will be easier to control. After attaching the pole end to the new guy, push that end forward (D).

Take the other end of the spinnaker pole off the old guy (it now becomes the sheet) and attach it to the mast (E, F). The jibe is now complete.

A Real-Life Jibe

Here's how a jibe works in real life, with the mainsail up. The forward crew gets ready with the pole; the middle crew has the spinnaker guy in one hand, the spinnaker sheet in the other; and the skipper steers while playing the mainsheet (A).

As the skipper turns the boat to leeward, the middle crew trims the guy and eases the sheet to keep the spinnaker square to the wind. The forward crew takes the pole off the mast and reaches for the new guy (B).

When the boat is heading directly downwind, the skipper uses the mainsheet to pull the boom across the boat. The forward crew attaches the spinnaker pole to the new guy (C).

Once the pole is attached to the new guy, the forward crew pushes that end forward to the clew. The middle crew keeps the spinnaker full (D).

The mainsail has now filled on the new jibe, and the forward crew attaches the end of the pole to the mast (E).

With the jibe complete, the crew return to their regular tasks and positions (F).

Two-Person Jibe

In a two-person boat, the roles are a bit different. When you begin to jibe, the crew hands the spinnaker sheet and guy to the skipper, who usually holds one in each hand and steers by straddling the tiller. The skipper must now steer the boat through the jibe as well as pull the spinnaker around the bow of the boat.

At the same time, the crew releases the twing on the old guy, tightens the twing on the new guy, and throws the boom over (in the middle of the jibe). Staying in the cockpit, the crew reaches around the front of the mast from the windward side, takes the spinnaker pole off the mast ring, and attaches it to the new guy. He or she then takes the pole off the old guy and attaches it to the mast.

As soon as the pole is in position, the crew cleats the guy and takes the spinnaker sheet from the skipper. You are now ready to take off again. As you can imagine, this maneuver takes a good deal of practice.

TAKEDOWNS

Dropping your spinnaker is often trickier than hoisting or jibing it; if you're not careful you'll end up seining for fish. We sailed an important race with Bill Ficker just after he won the 1970 America's Cup. We were in first place until we got to the leeward mark—when the spinnaker got a bit out of hand and filled with water about 50 yards behind the boat. Oops!

There are two basic ways to take your spinnaker down: on the windward side or on the leeward side. Each takedown has advantages in certain situations, so it is valuable to be familiar with both. No matter which way you drop the spinnaker, be sure the halyard and sheets are clear to run. The last thing you need is a knot when the spinnaker is halfway down.

Windward Takedown

On smaller boats (two or three people) this is the more common takedown. The forward crew first takes the pole off by detaching it from the mast, topping lift, and guy, in that order. As soon as the pole is removed and stored, the crew begins to gather in the spinnaker on the windward side. To do this, let the sheet go completely, pull on the guy, gather the foot of the spinnaker, and start pulling it down. Be sure someone remembers to drop the spinnaker halyard slowly.

In a two-person boat, the crew removes the spinnaker pole in the same manner, stores it, and then begins to gather in the spinnaker. If the spinnaker halyard is led back to the skipper, he or she lowers the spinnaker as the crew gathers it in; otherwise, the crew must lower the halyard while doing everything else.

Leeward Takedown

A leeward takedown is most commonly used on large boats where the spinnaker is too big to be muscled around to windward. Dropping the chute on the leeward side allows you to keep it in the wind shadow of the main, which makes it easier to handle. Leeward takedowns are seldom used on smaller boats in windy conditions because the crew would have to go to leeward, and this would heel the boat too much. It can, however, be an effective takedown in light air.

Begin the takedown with one crew to leeward, holding on to the spinnaker sheet. Then release the guy completely. At this moment, the crew to leeward gathers in the foot of the spinnaker. The other crew (or skipper) slowly lowers the halyard as the spinnaker is gathered. With a leeward takedown, the spinnaker pole can remain up indefinitely—until there is an opportunity to take it down. Just remember that you can't tack until it is lowered.

Both spinnaker takedowns will be easiest if the skipper heads the boat on a broad reach or run before you begin. This way you'll have the least possible wind pressure in the chute.

The Windward Takedown

A

B

C

When you are ready to take down the spinnaker, the first thing to do is to hoist the jib (A, B). To take the spinnaker down on the windward side, the forward crew must first take down the spinnaker pole (C). Take the pole off the mast first; then remove the topping lift hook from the middle of the pole; then remove the pole from the guy (D). While the forward crew stores the pole, the middle crew uses the guy to pull the spinnaker into the windward side

G

H

I

D

E

F

of the boat (E, F, G). Once the spinnaker is all bunched together, one of the crew should drop the spinnaker halyard (H). As the spinnaker comes down, stuff it neatly into the turtle or the cockpit (I, J). With the spinnaker down and stored, you are ready to assume normal sailing positions (K).

J

K

The Leeward Takedown

Another type of spinnaker drop is the leeward takedown. Like the windward takedown, it begins by hoisting the jib (A).

With a leeward drop, you lower the spinnaker before taking off the pole. While one crew member grabs the spinnaker sheet on the leeward side, the other lets the guy run free (B).

The spinnaker is then gathered on the leeward side (C).

Once the spinnaker is bunched together, the halyard is lowered slowly (D).

The spinnaker can be lowered right into the turtle so it is ready to be set again. The forward crew then removes the spinnaker pole whenever it is convenient (E).

8

Getting the Most from Your Sails

On a sailboat, your sails are your engine. Most small boats don't have motors, so you're dependent on the mainsail, jib, and spinnaker to get you where you want to go—and home again! That's why it's good to know how to set your sails so they make your boat move quickly. Efficient sail shape will also make your boat easier to handle—and therefore more fun—in all conditions.

Like the wings of a plane, sails are three-dimensional airfoils. Their shape is carefully designed to impart lift and to move a boat effectively on all points of sail. Unlike an airplane wing, however, the shape of a sail can be adjusted in order to get the most out of existing wind conditions.

VISUALIZING SAIL SHAPE

You don't have to be an aeronautical engineer to make your sails perform well, but there are a few things that are helpful to know. First, we usually describe the shape of a sail in two dimensions by viewing a horizontal cross-section from your position in the cockpit.

A boat's performance seems to be affected primarily by two components of a sail's shape: the amount of draft in the sail, and the position of that draft.

Sails are airfoils, and getting the most from them
requires a basic understanding of their optimum shape
when in use.

Amount of Draft

Draft is the amount of fullness, or curvature, in a sail. If a sail is flat as a board, then its cross-section is a straight line and it has no draft. You can measure the amount of draft in a sail in the following way:

1. Draw a straight line (CD) from luff to leech of the sail, parallel to the boom.

2. Find the point (E) where the sail is farthest away from this line. This is the position of maximum draft. From this point draw a perpendicular (EF) to your original line.

3. If you divide EF by CD, you get the amount of draft in the sail, expressed as a percentage of the sail's width. In most conditions, your sail will have a draft of about 15 percent. A sail with more draft than this would be called a "full" or "deep" sail; less draft produces a "flat" sail.

Position of Draft

Besides the amount of draft, we want to know where in the sail that draft is located. In other words, how far aft is the position of maximum draft (E) located? To find this, we divide CF by CD. In the ideal mainsail, the draft is located about 50 percent back in the sail. The draft in an ideal jib is about 40 percent back.

Since it's not a great idea to cut your sail in half in order to see its shape, this analysis is more helpful in theory than in practice. However, one thing racing sailors do to help them visualize sail shape while underway is to put "draft stripes" on their sail. Draft stripes are black lines that run across the mainsail or jib from luff to leech. They show the sail's shape as if you had cut the sail in half at that point.

Measuring Sail Shape

The shape of a sail is a key factor in boat performance and handling characteristics. It's usually easiest to visualize a sail in two dimensions, as if the sail were cut in half and you were viewing it in cross-section.

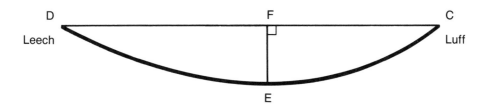

To determine the amount of fullness in a sail, draw the line CD and find the point where the sail is farthest from this line, E. Divide EF by CD to get the amount of fullness (expressed as a percentage).

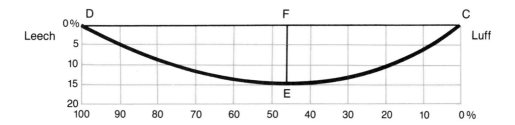

Besides the amount of fullness in a sail, it helps to know where that fullness is located. This position is usually expressed as a percentage of the distance from the luff to the leech.

HOW YOUR SAILS SHOULD LOOK

Now that you know how to describe the shape of a sail, you're ready to start optimizing your sail shape for various conditions. We've already given some rough numbers for average mainsail and jib shapes, but these vary with the amount of wind and the type of boat.

Catamarans and iceboats, for example, are always going fast, with their apparent wind very far ahead, so they have flat mainsails supported by full-length battens. In fact, their sails are quite like an airplane wing. (Plane wings don't have to change shape because they are always going about the same speed with the wind hitting them at the same angle.) In fact, some fast boats, like the *Stars & Stripes* catamaran, use "wing" sails, which are rigid.

Slower sailboats (including almost everything from Lasers to 12-Meters) are more sensitive to the shape of their airfoils. So to get top performance, you have to adjust sail shape according to conditions. Here is a general guide.

Light air. When the wind is light, a boat needs a lot of power from its sails. It must catch every bit of breeze to push the hull through the water. The sails, therefore, should be quite full.

Heavy air. Most boats get "overpowered" when the wind reaches about 15 knots, when they have all the wind power they can use. More power only heels the boat over more, which makes it slower and harder to control. In this situation, you have to start depowering by flattening the sails so the wind spills out of them easily. The windier it is, the flatter your sails should be.

Waves. When the water is rough, your boat is constantly being slowed as the bow plows into waves. What you need is a sail shape that's good for acceleration, so the boat will get going again after it hit each wave. The best shape for acceleration has the draft fairly far forward.

Upwind. When a boat is sailing into the wind, you want sails that are relatively flat. Flatter sails reduce drag when sailing upwind and also allow you to point a little closer to the wind.

Downwind. As soon as you stop sailing upwind and turn downwind, the ideal sail shape is much fuller. The wind is now starting to push the boat, and having more draft in your sails means you catch more wind.

How Your Sails Should Look

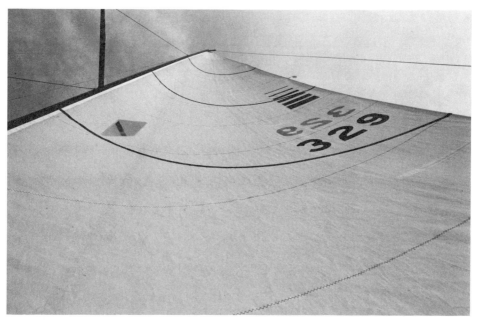

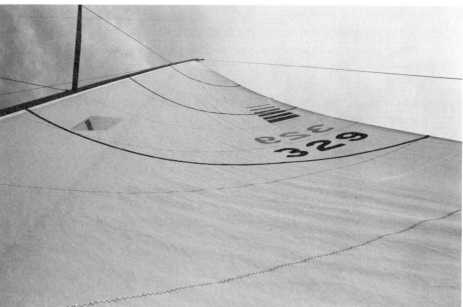

The sail at top is quite full, as can be seen by the curved draft stripes. The stripes are most curved near the luff, which means the position of the draft is forward. This would be a good shape for light air. The sail below is much flatter—the draft stripes are much straighter and not so curved in the front. This is a good heavy-air sail shape.

CONTROLLING SAIL SHAPE

Now that you have a rough idea of which sail shape is good for different conditions, how can you make your sails take that shape? Like an airline pilot, the skipper and crew of a sailboat have many controls at their fingertips.

Backstay. A number of larger one-designs (and almost all bigger boats) have adjustable backstays. The harder you pull on the backstay, the more you bend the mast and the flatter your mainsail gets. Pulling on the backstay also tightens the forestay, which flattens the jib. When you ease the backstay off again, you instantly add fullness and power to the sails.

Mainsheet. On boats without backstays, pulling on the mainsheet tightens the leech of the sail and actually controls mast bend. This makes the mainsail flatter. The mainsheet is a little like the gearshift on your car. When you ease it out, the sail gets full, the draft moves forward, and the boat accelerates. When you trim it in, you shift the mainsail into a flatter, pointing mode as the boat gets up to speed.

Outhaul. The outhaul controls fullness in the lower part of the mainsail. It should be tight for heavy air and eased off in lighter air and when going downwind.

Cunningham. When you pull on the cunningham (actually a downhaul on the luff of the mainsail), you flatten the mainsail and pull its draft forward. Like the outhaul, this control should be eased off all the way when going downwind to make the sail full.

Jib halyard. This control acts just like a cunningham on the jib, except it pulls up instead of down.

Traveler. The traveler allows you to control the athwartships position of the boom. In light air, pull the traveler above centerline so the boom can be centered without pulling too hard on the mainsheet. In heavy air, drop the traveler to spill wind and depower the sail.

Boom vang. The boom vang is used mostly in medium or heavy air when you are reaching or running. Without the vang on, the boom will tend to lift up in the air, which hurts sail shape and can be a little scary. Keep the vang on tight enough so the boom stays parallel to the deck when you ease the mainsheet.

SAIL TRIM

One objective when you're out sailing is to trim your sails efficiently so you get the best performance from your boat. To do this, it's helpful to have some

When sailing upwind, trim the traveler and mainsheet so the boom is roughly in the middle of the boat.

quick, dependable rules of thumb to follow. These will give you maximum performance with a minimum of effort.

Mainsail—Upwind

End of boom near the centerline. Trim the main in all the way so the end of the boom will be somewhere between the boat's centerline and the leeward corner of the transom.

Top batten parallel to boom. When the main is trimmed, the top batten should be roughly parallel to the boom. You can gauge this by sighting up from under the boom. If the batten hooks to windward, ease the mainsheet. If it falls off to leeward, trim the sheet.

Sail Trim—Mainsail Upwind

WIND

With the boom near the centerline when sailing upwind, trim the mainsheet so the top batten is parallel to the boom. In the photo at left, the top batten is twisted off to leeward, meaning the mainsheet should be trimmed tighter. In the center photo, the top batten is hooked to windward, so the mainsheet should be eased. Only in the photo at the right is the top batten parallel to the boom. This is the correct mainsail trim when sailing upwind.

Sail eased until it luffs along the mast. You'll get optimum downwind performance if you ease your main as far as possible. Ease the sheet until you see a bubble along the luff of the main, then trim it in slightly.

Vang tight enough so boom is horizontal. If it's windy, pull on your boom vang so it keeps the boom roughly horizontal and the upper batten parallel to the boom.

Telltale on top batten just flowing. Another good guide for downwind trim on a reach is to use the telltale (if you have one) on the end of the top batten. You want this telltale to fly as much as possible; if it's curling around behind the sail, try easing the vang or mainsheet a little.

Use the telltale on the end of the top batten as a guide for mainsail trim. In general, you should keep the telltale flying for both upwind sailing and reaching. If it stalls, try easing the mainsheet or boom vang.

Jib—Upwind

Middle batten parallel to centerline. Just like the main, the jib should be trimmed in all the way for sailing upwind. If you have battens along the leech of your jib, you want them to be roughly parallel to the boat's centerline.

Even, consistent curve in slot between main and jib. When you look at the "slot" (the space between the leech of the jib and the leeward side of the main) from the stern of your boat, you should see similar curves in both the main and the jib. If you don't, try moving the jib lead athwartships.

Telltales flutter simultaneously from top to bottom. The fore and aft position of the jib lead is important for top performance. Ideally, the telltales along the luff of the jib should all move simultaneously. If the top telltales flutter first, move your jib lead forward, and vice versa.

Jib—Downwind

Don't fly jib and spinnaker simultaneously. On most boats, you should drop the jib so it won't take wind away from the spinnaker. This is more important in light air than in heavy air.

Ease sail until telltales start to break. If you don't set a spinnaker, ease the jib as far as possible until the windward telltales start to flutter or the front of the jib begins luffing.

Move jib leads farther outboard (or "wing" the sail). The jib leads should be as far outboard as possible for downwind sailing. If you're on a run, you can "wing" the jib to the windward side to help keep it filled (see page 102).

Spinnaker

Spinnakers are free-flying creatures that change shape continually. Unlike the main and jib, which are attached along one entire edge, spinnakers are fixed at only two points—the head and the tack (at the spinnaker pole). For this reason, spinnaker aerodynamics have always been a bit mysterious, even to the best sailors and sailmakers.

In spite of this mystery, there are a few guidelines for trimming your spinnaker so it pulls the boat as quickly as possible. Some of these were covered in the last chapter, but let's review them quickly. First, pull your spinnaker pole aft until it is roughly perpendicular to the true wind. Second, adjust the height of the pole (with the topping lift) so the two clews of the spinnaker are level.

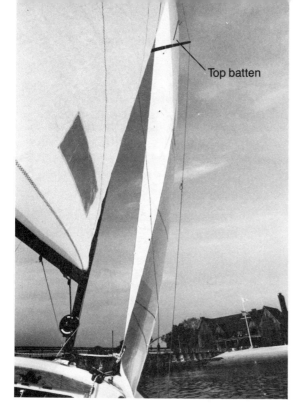

Top batten

Sail Trim— Jib: Upwind

Like the main, the jib should be trimmed so the top batten (shown here with a dark stripe just above the spreader) is parallel to the centerline of the boat. This jib could be trimmed in slightly.

Leeward spreader

Leech

Slot

Position the jib leads so the "slot" between the mainsail and jib has an even, consistent curve. One good guide for trimming the jib is to use the position of the leech relative to the leeward spreader.

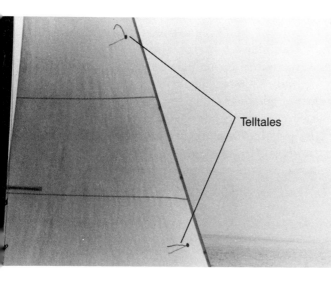

Telltales

Use the telltales along the luff of the jib to set the fore and aft position of the jib leads. The goal is to have all the telltales move simultaneously. If the upper ones luff first (as shown here), move the jib lead forward to trim the top part of the sail tighter.

Third, always ease the spinnaker sheet until the luff of the sail begins to curl slightly.

If weather conditions get windy, most spinnakers can turn into a handful, especially if you're inexperienced. Here are a few things you can do to keep the chute (and your boat) under control:

Move the spinnaker sheet lead forward. This "chokes down" the spinnaker and keeps it from oscillating back and forth.

Over-square the pole. In other words, trim the guy more than you would normally. This makes the bottom part of the spinnaker flatter and keeps it steady.

Move your crew weight aft. This keeps the spinnaker from pulling the bow down into the water, which would make the boat "squirrely" (hard to keep under control).

Head up a little higher toward the wind. This works very well when you are going dead downwind and the boat starts to roll back and forth.

SOLVING COMMON TRIMMING PROBLEMS

Sometimes when you're sailing along, you look up at the sails and you know that something isn't right. You may not be sure exactly what, but you know that there's probably something you could do to make your sails perform better. Let's look at some potential problems:

Bubble in the front of the main. A bubble in the main is caused by backwind from the jib. You will always have a little bubble when sailing upwind, especially in heavy air. If the backwind seems excessive, however, it means that your jib is overtrimmed or your main is not trimmed in enough.

Lots of wrinkles. Wrinkles in a sail aren't necessarily bad. They don't look too great, but a few wrinkles here and there won't significantly affect boat performance. If your sail has unsightly wrinkles, however, there are several things you can do. First, check to be sure your sail is pulled all the way to the top of the mast. Second, straighten out your mast by easing the backstay and/or vang. And third, try pulling on the cunningham.

Leech flutters. Sometimes the leech of your main or jib will flap obnoxiously in the breeze, sounding something like an engine. This is not good for the sail because it quickly damages the cloth. However, this condition is common on older sails, and there is often not a lot you can do to prevent it. If you're

Two Common Sail-Trim Problems

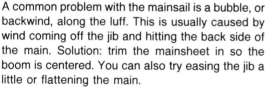

A common problem with the mainsail is a bubble, or backwind, along the luff. This is usually caused by wind coming off the jib and hitting the back side of the main. Solution: trim the mainsheet in so the boom is centered. You can also try easing the jib a little or flattening the main.

Another problem with the main is unsightly wrinkles. Sometimes these can be removed simply by pulling harder on the cunningham. Other times, however, they mean you have too much mast bend (as is the case here). Solution: ease the mainsheet, backstay, and/or boom vang.

sailing a bigger boat, check to see if your sail has a leechline running up inside the leech. If it does, tighten this line.

Leech hooks. The leech of your main may hook to windward. This is another common problem with older sails. The only thing you can do is refrain from trimming the sheet too hard. If your sail has a leechline, see if this line needs to be eased.

Spinnaker collapses. A collapsing spinnaker is a sign that your sail is being trimmed incorrectly. Tell your trimmer to pull the sheet a little harder and not to let the luff of the spinnaker curl so much. You may also want to ease the guy forward a little.

Another concern is what to do when it's windy and things start getting a little out of control. Learning to sail in a breeze usually requires time in the boat, but you can shape your sails to make life a little easier. First of all, make your sails as flat as possible. Pull the backstay very tight. Then tighten the outhaul, cunningham, and jib halyard quite a bit. Let the traveler slide to leeward, and move the jib leads outboard and aft. Put the vang on just tight enough to keep the boom from flying up in the air.

Be sure to keep the mainsheet and jib sheets in hand at all times. Don't cleat them! Keep these sheets eased enough so that the boat doesn't heel too much, and be ready to ease them further if you get a puff. Depowering the sails like this will make your boat a lot easier and more fun to sail when it's windy. If the breeze starts blowing hard, don't hesitate to drop your jib and sail with the main alone. Just watch out, because it's a little easier to get caught in irons this way.

TAKING CARE OF YOUR SAILS

Sails play an important role on your boat and they're relatively fragile, so it's important to take special care with them. This will help prevent damage and extend the life of the sail (thereby saving you money).

When you're out sailing, avoid flogging your sails whenever possible. In other words, unless you have a good reason, don't just let the sails flap in the breeze. This is one of the fastest ways to break down the sail material.

Be sure you take good care of your sails when they aren't on the boat as well. The best way to put sails away is to roll them. This avoids creasing the sail, which eventually breaks down sailcloth. Many sailmakers supply "sausage" bags to hold their rolled sails. If you don't roll your sails, the next best alternative is folding.

Every few times you go sailing, wash the sails with fresh water and let them dry completely before storing. Always wash the sails before putting them away for the winter. When storing your sails, make sure that you protect them from the sun. If you leave your mainsail on the boom, use a cover. Ultraviolet degradation is another quick way to break down sailcloth.

Storing Your Sails

Rolling.
Rolling is the best way to store a sail. Begin rolling the sail from the head, with the foot still on the boom. With one person guiding each side of the sail, roll straight along the leech so the roll stays parallel to the battens. Once you reach the foot, slide the sail off the boom straight into the bag.

Folding.
If you are going to fold the sail, you can do so right on top of the boom (left) to save the bother of rerigging it the next time you sail, or you can fold it on a clean, flat surface (such as the dock, below). Remember to avoid folding on the same creases every time, and keep the leech together as you fold so the battens will be together when you fold the sail in thirds to put it in the bag.

Ultraviolet rays are one of the worst enemies of any sail. Therefore, if you leave your sail on the boom, be sure to protect it with a cover.

9

Seamanship

The ability to handle a boat skillfully and safely in a wide range of conditions is known as seamanship. Seamanship covers almost everything under the sun, from knot tying to docking to handling a vicious squall. We obviously don't have room to cover every possible subject here, so we will concentrate on those areas that will be most helpful to aspiring small-boat sailors.

AVOIDING COLLISIONS

Hitting another boat is one of the biggest fears of beginning sailors. Fortunately, there are very clear right-of-way rules that explain which boat must keep clear in any situation. When you understand these rules, a mishap is much less likely.

The most commonly used rules of the road are the Inland Rules, which apply to coastal waters, lakes, and rivers. COLREGS, the International Regulations for Preventing Collisions at Sea, are in effect in outer coastal waters and on the high seas. In essence, these two systems are almost the same, although there are slight differences in the wording of some rules and in the appropriate signals that boats must make. We will discuss only the Inland Rules here. If you will be sailing offshore, be sure to familiarize yourself with COLREGS.

Like the laws about driving a car, the purpose of boating rules is to prevent collisions. You wouldn't want to go for a drive in your car and have some people driving on the right and others on the left. The same thing would happen with boats if everyone didn't obey common rules.

There is one basic principle underlying all right-of-way rules: When two boats approach, one boat, the "give-way" boat, is responsible for altering course to stay clear of the other boat, the "stand-on" (or "right-of-way") boat. In order

153

Knowing the rules of the road is one of the many important aspects of seamanship.

for the give-way boat to have a predictable obstacle to avoid, the stand-on boat must maintain her course and speed. The one exception to this, of course, is if she must take last-minute evasive action to avoid a collision.

Here are some of the most pertinent Inland Rules.

1. A moving boat must stay clear of a boat not moving.

2. Large unmaneuverable boats, such as freighters, ferryboats, or tugs with barges, have right of way over boats less than 20 meters long and over all sailboats in narrow channels and in traffic separation zones.

3. Because they are more maneuverable, powerboats must give way to sailboats in open water.

4. Between two sailboats: If they are on the same tack, the windward boat must stay clear; if they're on opposite tacks, the port tack boat must stay clear.

5. When two powerboats (including a sailboat under power) meet head to head, the preferred course is to pass port side to port side (like cars).

6. An overtaking boat (approaching from within 67.5 degrees of dead astern) must stay clear of the boat it is overtaking.

7. If two boats under power are on crossing courses (not head to head or overtaking), the boat on the left (give-way) must stay clear, preferably by passing astern of the boat on the right (stand-on). If you are unsure about this rule, there's an easy way to remember it: just look over at the running lights on the boat you are approaching. If you see the green light (starboard side), it means you can keep going. If you see the red light (port side), it means you should stop and give them the right of way.

When boats are racing, an entirely different set of rules, called the International Yacht Racing Rules, are in effect. We will discuss these in Chapter 12.

When you are converging with another boat, there are two very reliable ways to predict the likelihood of collision. First, look at the land behind the bow of the other boat. If the boat is staying in the same place relative to the land, then you are on a collision course. If the land appears to be moving one way or the other, then you will probably miss each other. If there is no land visible behind the other boat, you can use your compass to take a bearing. If the other boat holds a constant bearing, you are on a collision course. If you are gaining bearing, you will pass ahead; if you are losing bearing, the other boat will cross ahead.

Navigation lights are required on all moving boats after sunset. The number and position of the lights vary according to the type and size of boat, but the most common are the red (port) and green (starboard) side lights and the white stern light. These lights are positioned so sailors can determine who are the give-way and stand-on boats.

Avoiding Collisions

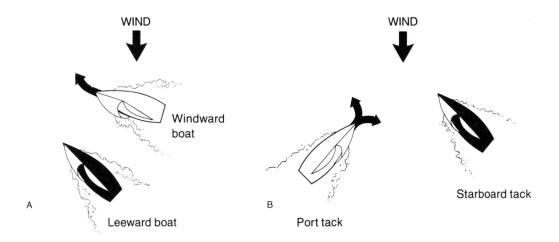

The Inland Rules define which boat must keep clear when two boats converge. If the boats are on the same tack (A), the windward boat must stay clear. If they are on opposite tacks (B), the boat on port tack must stay clear.

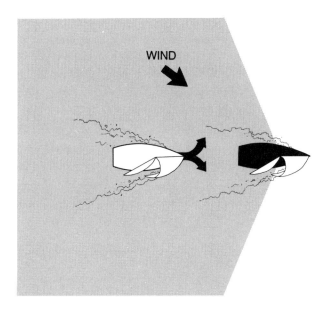

According to the Inland Rules, an overtaking boat (white) must stay clear of the boat it is overtaking. This rule applies to any boat approaching from within 67.5 degrees of dead astern (shaded area).

Avoiding Collisions (Cont.)

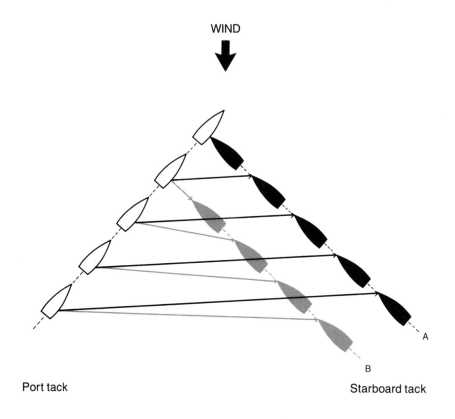

WIND

Port tack

Starboard tack

A

B

When you are on port tack (white), you must stay clear of a boat on starboard tack (black and grey). In this situation, it's important to know whether you will cross ahead of the other boat or not. One good way to tell is to take a compass bearing on the other boat. If this bearing remains constant (A), then you are on a collision course. If you "gain bearing," however, then you will cross ahead (B).

For example, if you see a stern light ahead, you may be overtaking. When you see a green side light, the other boat is to your left and must give way; when you see a red side light, you must give way. If you see both red and green lights, the other boat is headed straight at you.

LAUNCHING YOUR BOAT

Getting your boat into the water can sometimes be more of a problem than sailing it. After many years of launching small boats, we can say with certainty that we've caused more damage while getting our boats in and out of the water than we have while sailing. Therefore, a bit of caution and know-how is advisable.

On a Ramp

If you are launching from a ramp, you can rig your boat completely while it is still on the trailer—but wait to hoist the sails. Undo all the tie-down lines except for the bow line. Slowly back down the ramp until the boat is in deep enough water to float. The car should *not* be in the water; if it is, consider getting a trailer tongue extender. Once the boat is afloat, untie the bow line, pull the boat clear of the trailer, and pull the trailer out of the water.

On a Hoist

Check to be sure you know how to operate the hoist, and never exceed the marked weight limit. Move your boat into position so it is centered under the hoist. Often there will be a line painted on the pavement, based on the swing of the hoist arm, to indicate where the center of your boat should be. Use a bridle that has sufficient strength and holds the boat level as it lifts off the trailer. It's o.k. to have the bow down slightly so the mast doesn't hit the hoist.

As the hoist begins to raise the boat, check to be sure that all the hooks are clear (also be sure your bailers are closed). Someone should be holding onto a bow and a stern line so the boat will not swing around and hit the trailer. Swing the hoist over the water and lower the boat. *Never* stand underneath the boat.

Launching Your Boat

On a ramp.

When launching your boat on a ramp, the key is to back it slowly until the boat is in deep enough water to float. Though these young women have raised the boat's jib before launching, they have left the jib sheets unfastened so that the jib will merely luff should a breeze come up during the actual launch.

On a hoist.

As the person on the right pulls the hoist and boat over the water, the person on the left holds a bow line to prevent the boat from swinging wildly. Note that the lifting bridle has been rigged to keep the mast away from the hoist arm.

GETTING OUT TO THE SAILING AREA

Once your boat is in the water, you still have to get out to the sailing area. This is often a challenge in itself, depending on wind conditions, the ability of your crew, and the number of obstacles in your way.

Leaving the Dock

If the wind is pushing you away from the dock, departure is easy. Keep your bow line attached and let the boat swing away from the dock so it is headed into the wind. Then raise your sails. Have someone on the dock push your bow to one side, or back your jib so the bow goes one way. You're off!

Leaving the dock under sail is more difficult with the wind blowing onto the dock. If you have an outboard, push your bow off the dock and motor away from it before going head to wind to raise your sails. Without an outboard, you'll have to raise your sails at the dock and sail away. Just be sure your mainsheet and jib sheets are free, so the sails will luff completely when you hoist them. Then push the bow off the dock and trim the main to help you steer away from the dock.

Leaving a Mooring

Sailing away from a mooring is simple because the boat will naturally swing so the bow is pointed into the wind. The only potential problem is wrapping the mooring line around your centerboard or rudder. Once you've raised the sails, pull yourself forward on the mooring line and back the jib to push the bow away from the mooring. Then trim your sails. Be sure you have enough forward momentum for steerage before you let go of the mooring.

Towing a Boat

Sometimes you need a tow from another boat to get out to the sailing area. For this reason, you should always carry a towline of sufficient strength and length. This is a safety precaution as well, in case you capsize or get caught in a squall and need to be towed.

Your towline should be led through a lead on the bow, then tied around the base of the mast. Cleats on the bow are meant for docking, not for towing, so don't use them unless you want to rip out your deck. Don't ever tie the towline around your forestay.

Keep your crew weight aft while being towed to prevent the bow from plowing. And if you have a centerboard, it should be raised about halfway while under tow.

Towing.
When your boat is being towed behind a motorboat, tie your towline around the mast with a bowline. Raise the centerboard halfway, and keep your crew weight centered toward the stern of the boat.

Once you've successfully launched your boat and had a lovely sail, your final challenge is returning to the dock or mooring.

Docking

The most common mistake is coming into a dock with too much speed, usually because sailors approach the dock on a downwind course. Many times we've seen a crew member stick an arm or leg out to stop the boat from crashing into the dock. This can be really dangerous!

The key to any landing maneuver is to approach as slowly as possible, while still maintaining enough forward motion for steerage. Approach the dock on a course that is nearly parallel to it. It is critical to consider the effects of the wind and current in your approach. For example, it is preferable to land on the leeward side of the dock. And you always want to land so your bow is pointed into the wind and current (or the combined effect of the two) as much as possible. That way, they will help you slow down.

When docking, you have to be able to use your sails to control your speed. Try to approach the dock on a close reach so you can luff the sails to slow down or trim them to speed up. If you land straight downwind, you won't be able to slow enough. If you land straight into the wind, you risk losing way before you reach the dock. Once you reach the dock, secure the bow line, drop the sails, then throw a stern line.

Sometimes your only option is to come in on the windward side of the dock or with the wind astern. In these instances, drop your sails when you are directly upwind of the dock and let the wind slowly push you in. *Never* attempt to land on a broad reach or a run with your sails up.

Mooring

Approaching a mooring is very similar to approaching a dock, except that it's much easier to avoid crashing. You want to approach slowly from the down-wind (or down-current) side, using your sails to control your speed. The basic procedure is to sail to leeward of the mooring, then go head to wind and coast to a stop right as you reach the mooring buoy. If you're going a little too fast, back the main (by pushing it out to one side) to slow the boat down. Of course, all this takes a bit of practice!

Docking Your Boat

Always approach a dock from the downwind side. Sail toward the dock on a close reach so you can luff the sails to control your speed (A).

A

Here the boat has a lot of momentum, so the crew is luffing both sails to slow the approach to the dock (B).

B

The skipper starts turning the boat to come alongside the dock. Whenever possible, you should land at the dock with your bow pointing into the wind (C, D).

C

D

By the time the bow reaches the dock, the boat should be moving very slowly. One crew member prepares to fend off and step onto the dock (E, F).

E

F

This crew has done an excellent job of slowing the boat and bringing it into the dock. As a result, all the crew member has to do is step onto the dock and hold the boat (G).

G

A successful docking is a calm and relaxed affair (H).

H

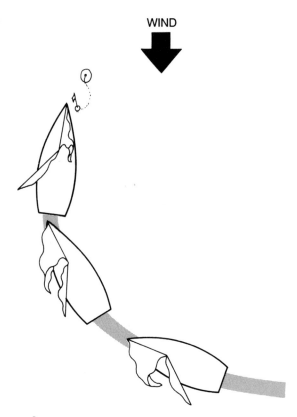

WIND

Picking up a mooring.
Picking up a mooring is a lot like landing at a dock. Always approach from the downwind side, and come in on a reach so you can luff the sails to control your speed. Make your final approach upwind, so you can use the wind to slow the boat. You can even back the main to kill some speed. The great thing about a mooring is that if you miss it, you can always circle around and try again.

Landing on a Beach or Ramp

Boats with centerboards and flip-up rudders can easily land on a beach. But don't try this if you are worried about the smooth finish of your bottom, since sand is not kind to gel coat. Approach a beach or ramp as you would a dock, lowering your sails first if the wind is blowing onshore. Be sure to raise your centerboard and rudder before they hit bottom. Then hop overboard and walk your boat to the beach. If waves are breaking, landing on a beach is not advisable.

RUNNING AGROUND

Running aground is never desirable, but fortunately it is usually not too much of a problem in a small boat (unless you crash into rocks). The best way to avoid this situation is to prevent it by careful observation of navigational aids (see below). Even with the best intentions, however, you will probably feel the bottom sooner or later. We can't count all the times we've run aground in a sailboat.

If you do run aground, the first thing to do is to raise the centerboard and turn away from the shallow area. A keelboat obviously has a more serious problem, but you may be able to free yourself by heeling the boat over (with crew weight) to reduce draft. If there is a motorboat nearby, you can often talk them into helping. Or you may be able to jump overboard and walk your boat into deeper water. If the tide is coming in, you can simply wait for the higher water to float you free; but if the tide is dropping, do everything possible to get free immediately.

KNOTS

Knots are usually the most boring part of any sailing instruction, so we'll cover only the basics you really need. Keep in mind, however, that knowing a few essential knots will make your sailing much more convenient and safe.

Bowline. The bowline is perhaps the most important all-around knot. It's used to tie loops in lines such as docking lines, jib sheets, and towlines. One of the great things about a bowline is that it's very easy to undo, even after it has been pulled very tight.

Figure eight. The figure eight is a simple knot tied in the end of sheets and sail control lines to prevent them from pulling through a block, grommet, or cleat.

Clove hitch. The clove hitch is used to attach a line to a post or a spar; uses include tying a docking line to a piling or a fender to a lifeline.

Square knot. The square knot is used to tie together two ends of a line, and most commonly is used in tying up a furled sail. Be careful when tying this so you don't get a granny (the knot in your kid's shoelaces that is impossible to undo).

Knots

There are several knots you really need to know for everyday sailing on a small boat. These include the bowline, the figure eight, the square knot, and the clove hitch.

Bowline   Figure eight

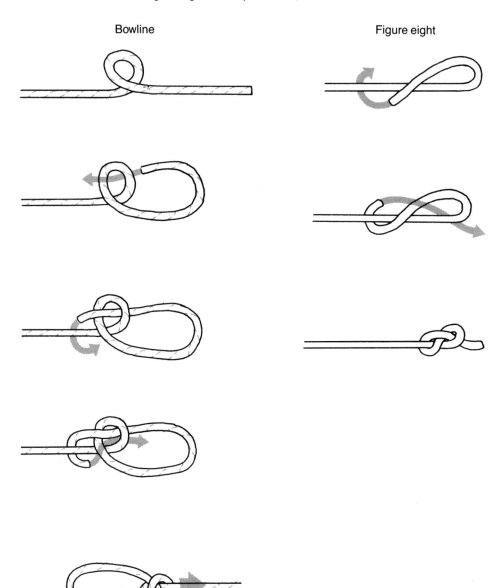

Square knot   Clove hitch

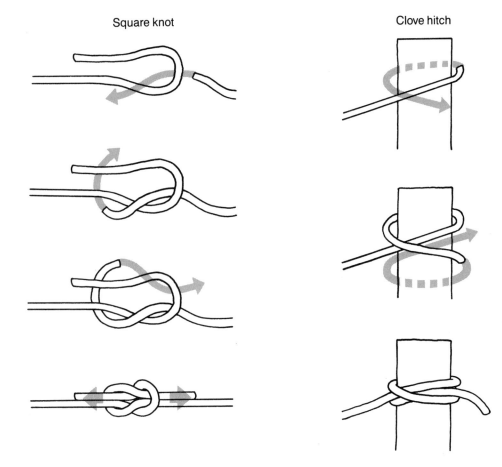

NAVIGATION

Simply put, navigation is the art of getting your boat from one place to another safely. There's nothing worse than going out for a sail and getting lost or running aground.

Charts

Next to your own observation, charts and a compass are the most important tools of navigation. Charts show everything you need to know about a body of water, including the depths (in feet or fathoms at mean low water), bottom characteristics, features on shore, aids to navigation, latitude, longitude, and true and magnetic compass directions. Distance on the water is measured in terms of nautical miles; one nautical mile is 6,076 feet (a statute mile is 5,280 feet).

Other important information about tides, danger areas, weather, and storm warnings is also found on most charts. Since charts are usually made of paper and are reasonably expensive, you will want to take good care of them by rolling (instead of folding), using a pencil (instead of a pen), and protecting them from water.

Aids to Navigation

The most common navigational aids are the buoys that mark channels, shoals, and obstructions. The important feature of these buoys is their color. In the United States, there is a system for the way buoys are laid out, based on entering from seaward. When you are going from a larger body of water to a smaller one, such as when you enter a harbor from a bay, you are considered to be "returning." When you are returning, you leave red buoys to starboard (on your right) and green buoys to port. The common saying is "Red right returning." The buoys are also numbered, starting with "1" at the channel entrance and getting higher as you go in. Green buoys are odd-numbered and red buoys are even.

In a larger body of water, buoys may mark shoals or obstructions, rather than a specific channel, but if you have an overview of the body of water you are sailing on and the direction you are going, you can determine whether you are "returning" or not, and therefore know which side to leave a buoy by its color. A green-and-red-striped buoy is called a "mid-channel marker" and can be passed on either side, although the top color indicates the preferred side.

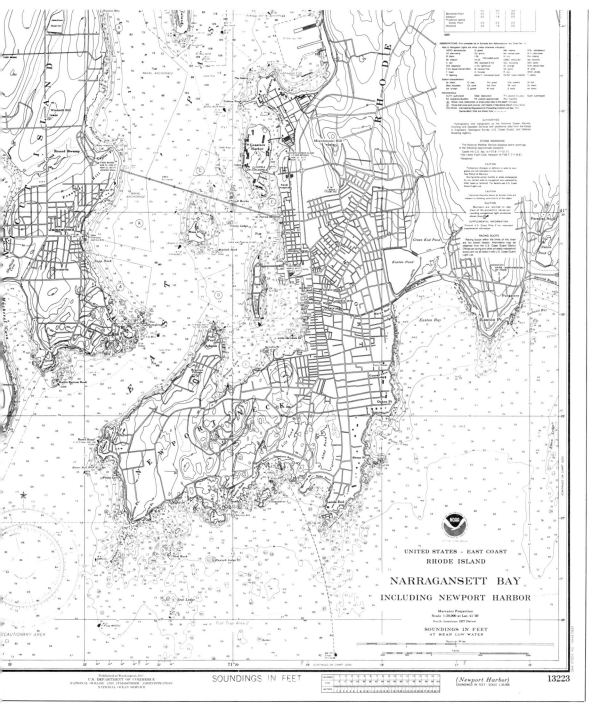

A portion of a typical government chart, in this case of Rhode Island's Narragansett Bay.
Careful study of any chart will reveal an incredible amount of useful information.

Buoys

The three most common buoys in use today are bellbuoys (left), "nuns" (center), and "cans" (right). Nuns are painted red, cans green. When returning to a harbor, you should pass red buoys on your right (starboard), green buoys on your left (port).

Lights, reflectors, sounds, and shape are other characteristics that help identify buoys. Green buoys have green or white lights and a green reflector strip. Red buoys have red or white lights and a red reflector. The light can be fixed or flashing in a specific pattern, which will be indicated on the chart. Important buoys also have sound signals—a bell, gong, horn, or whistle. The bell has one tone; the gong has several. Finally, the shape is indicative of the buoy's color, with "cans" (flat tops) always being green and "nuns" (pointed tops) being red.

Lighthouses are other major aids to navigation. Built on prominent points of land or offshore platforms, they have very high bright lights that can be seen from quite a distance. As with buoys, the lights have specific characteristics, which are listed on the chart. The chart will also indicate the height of the light (above mean high water), the distance from which it is visible (on a clear day), and any sound signals or radio transmissions from it.

Compass

A compass consists of a set of magnets attached to the underside of a compass card. The magnets align with the earth's magnetic field, and the compass card shows the direction the boat is heading relative to magnetic north. The magnets and card balance on a pin and are housed inside a dome that is filled with a liquid that dampens the effects of the boat's movement on the card. Note that there are two different compass roses on every chart. The outside one is based on true north, while the inside one refers to magnetic north. You should use the inside one for all your navigation.

These are the basic tools you'll be using in navigating a small sailboat, but of course there are many more. If you decide to take a longer journey on a bigger boat, consult one of the many excellent books on navigation.

10

Weather, Wind, and Current

The sport of sailing is probably more dependent on natural elements than is any other human activity. Sailboats and sailors are entirely at the mercy of wind and waves, not to mention sun, heat, cold, current, and splashing water. The ability to predict and handle a variety of weather conditions will make sailing more fun for you—and safer. While cruisers and day sailors don't have the sophisticated weather technology of an America's Cup syndicate, anyone who goes out on the water in a sailboat still should know as much about the weather as possible.

WEATHER: THE BIG PICTURE

What are the causes of weather and wind? Weather is actually movement and change in the bottom layer of the atmosphere. This layer is directly affected by differences in temperature and pressure caused by the effects of the sun on the varying surfaces of the Earth, as well as by the angle and intensity of the sun. When air is warmed over land or at the Equator, for example, it expands and rises, creating an area of lower pressure. Cooler air over water or in the polar regions contracts and creates higher pressure. High-pressure areas typically move toward areas of low pressure. This movement is one cause of wind.

The lower atmosphere is made up of a series of air masses, each of which has its own characteristics of temperature, pressure, and water content. Maritime air masses form over the oceans and are usually high in moisture. Continental air masses form over land and are much drier. Depending on where an air mass has formed and traveled, it can be warm or cool. Within each air mass the weather is relatively steady, but when different air masses interact, we get changes in the weather.

173

Being able to predict weather conditions is a requisite for safe sailing.

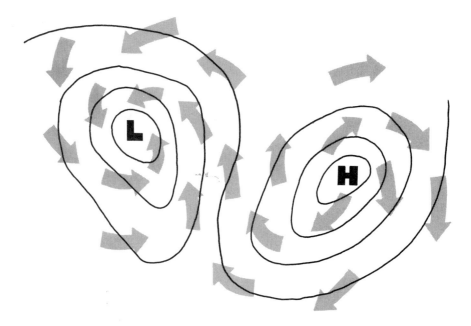

Isobars.
Large-scale weather maps are drawn like topographic maps. The isobars show where there is equal atmospheric pressure. When the isobars are close together, the weather will change rapidly. In general, the wind flows clockwise around high-pressure areas and counterclockwise around low-pressure areas. It also flows from high-pressure areas to low-pressure areas.

Atmospheric pressure can be plotted with isobars (lines of equal pressure), just as a topographical map shows the contours of the earth's surface. High-pressure areas can be thought of as mountains, for there is more dense air pushing down, while low-pressure areas are like valleys. When the isobar lines are very close together, you have a "cliff," which means unsettled weather.

In general, wind flows from the mountains to the valleys. Because of the Coriolis force (caused by the spinning of the Earth), the wind flows clockwise around high-pressure areas in the Northern Hemisphere, and counterclockwise in the Southern Hemisphere. Conversely, the wind flows counterclockwise around low-pressure areas in the Northern Hemisphere, and clockwise in the Southern Hemisphere.

Fronts

When two air masses come together, the boundary is often a confused and unsettled area called a *front*. A cold front occurs when cooler, drier air wedges in under warmer moist air. It is usually fast moving and is often marked by a line of thunderstorms. The cumulonimbus (thunderstorm) clouds building high above the front are a warning signal that danger is near.

A warm front approaches more gradually as warm, moist air slowly moves in over cooler, drier air. High-level cirrus clouds usually indicate the approach of the warm front within a couple of days. The cirrus clouds are followed by lower and thicker clouds as the front gets nearer, until thick nimbostratus clouds bring extensive precipitation. Unlike the cold front, however, the passage of a warm front is usually not stormy.

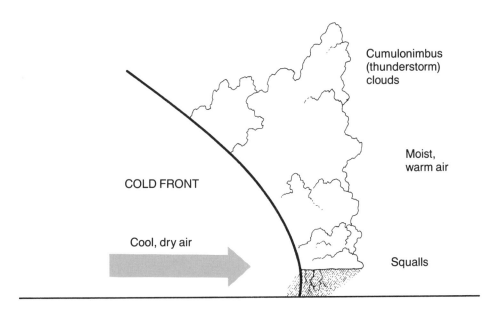

Cold fronts.
A cold front approaches rapidly and brings a quick, often violent, change in weather. The usual warning signs of a cold front are high thunderstorm clouds in the west.

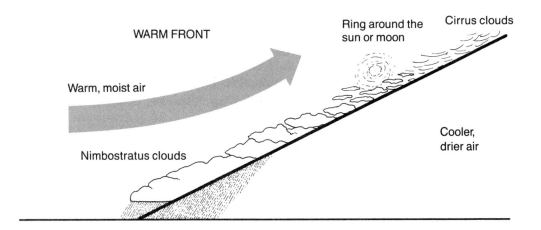

Warm fronts.
In sharp contrast to a cold front, a warm front brings a slow, gradual change in the weather. While you can generally expect rain with a warm front, it is not usually stormy like a cold front.

When you are on the water, there are a number of signs you can use to predict the weather.

Watch the west. In the Northern Hemisphere, the weather pattern generally moves from west to east. This means that if you want to know what type of weather is on the way, look toward the west.

Clouds. Clouds are often the best way to tell what's coming. Here are some of the most common types:

Cumulus: puffy white clouds that typically form over land during fair weather. They often mean you can expect a sea breeze.

Cirrus: very high, stringy clouds made of ice crystals, usually indicating the slow approach of a warm front; sometimes called "mare's tails."

Altocumulus: wavy ridges of clouds looking a bit like fish scales, indicating that a warm front is getting closer; also known as a "mackerel sky."

Stratus: very low gray rain clouds.

Nimbostratus: very low, dark gray spread-out rain clouds.

Cirrostratus: high, whitish stratus clouds, darker and thicker than white cirrus.

Cumulonimbus: tall, imposing thunderheads that often indicate the approach of a cold front.

Halos. A large halo, or ring, appearing around the sun or the moon is caused by high cirrostratus clouds at the beginning of a warm front; it is frequently followed by lower, thicker clouds and then rain.

Sunrises and sunsets. "Red sky in the morning, sailor take warning; red sky at night, sailor's delight." This old saying usually holds true. Red light is created when the sun's rays hit dust particles in clear, dry air. A red sunset, therefore, means that there is clear, dry air coming. A red sky in the morning, however, indicates that the clear weather has already passed.

These are just a few of the ways that we, as amateur meteorologists, can predict weather while we're on the water. If you want a more accurate forecast or a report before you go sailing, try a professional weather service.

Clouds

All good sailors should be able to recognize the seven cloud patterns shown here, and know what kind of weather each portends.

Cumulus   Stratus   Nimbostratus   Cumulonimbus

Altocumulus   Cirrostratus   Cirrus

OBTAINING WEATHER INFORMATION

Television, newspapers, and radio reports can give you a general prediction for the day. Some use detailed weather maps showing isobars and fronts; others, however, seem more concerned with Nielsen ratings than with the actual weather. In either case, the information is large scale and usually not very detailed about the sailing conditions in your local area.

The National Weather Service broadcasts continuous weather reports over VHF frequencies 162.400, 162.475, and 162.550 megahertz. They give the present wind strength and direction, temperature, sea conditions, visibility, and tides in your area, as well as information on the movement of fronts, precipitation, and fog. They also give local and regional forecasts for the next 24 hours, plus an extended forecast. Advisories or warnings are broadcast, and thunderstorms are tracked.

Many marinas and yacht clubs post visual weather warnings to alert boaters to adverse weather conditions. You may see:

One triangular red flag: small-craft warning (winds 18 to 33 knots)

Two triangular red flags: gale warning (winds 33 to 47 knots)

One square red-and-black flag: storm warning (winds 48 to 63 knots)

Two square red-and-black flags: hurricane warning (winds greater than 64 knots)

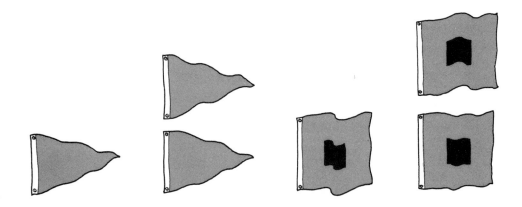

Signal flags.
When you see any of the following signals displayed at your local yacht club or marina, it's usually a good idea to do something other than sail a small boat.

If you ever see two red-and-black flags flying at your local club, batten the hatches and head for home.

Other sources of weather information include local airports, flight service stations (for pilots), and weather facsimile machines that draw synoptic maps. Perhaps the most valuable source is your own experience and observation. Learn what the weather patterns are in your sailing area by observing the clouds, barometric pressure, temperature, wind direction and speed, and humidity. We keep notebooks that include a record of the weather and what the wind does every day we go sailing.

HOW WEATHER AFFECTS WIND

As we have seen, wind is caused by air moving from areas of high pressure to areas of low pressure. The greater the difference in the pressure, the stronger the wind will be. The direction of the wind in your sailing area will depend on two things: (1) the positions and movements of pressure areas and (2) local thermal effects. Here are some of the basic types of breezes:

High pressure. A high-pressure system generally brings cooler air from the north. You've seen this many times on crisp, clear fall days when there's a chill in the air and the leaves are blowing all over. This breeze usually blows from the northwest and is very puffy and shifty.

Low pressure. A storm system typically brings winds from the east. These winds are usually very strong and steady, and are typically accompanied by rain and higher tides.

Sea breeze. This is a very common breeze in shore areas, caused by differences between the land and water temperatures. During the day, the sun heats the land more quickly than the water, causing the air to rise above the land. This draws in cooler air from over the water. As this moist air moves over land, it gets hotter and rises, forming cumulus clouds. In order to have a strong sea breeze on the surface, there must be a gradient wind aloft in a direction opposing the sea breeze. This carries the heated moist air out over the water where it cools and subsides, rejoining the thermal cycle.

Land breeze. As evening approaches and the sun goes down, the land radiates its heat until it is cooler than the water. This creates higher pressure over land, so air begins to flow out to the lower-pressure area over the water. This breeze is not nearly as strong as the sea breeze because the temperature differences between the land and the water are not as great at night.

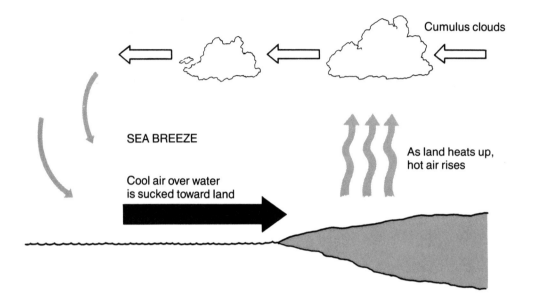

Cumulus clouds

SEA BREEZE

As land heats up,
hot air rises

Cool air over water
is sucked toward land

The sea breeze.
One of the most common types of sailing wind is the sea breeze. This wind, which can be
quite strong, is produced when hot air rises off the land and sucks in the cool ocean air
underneath. This thermal breeze is responsible for the great sailing conditions in such places
as San Francisco Bay; Fremantle, Australia; and Buzzards Bay in New England.

WIND CHARACTERISTICS

One thing you will learn about the wind is that it's always changing. Even when
the breeze seems very steady, an experienced sailor will pick up subtle changes
in velocity and direction. Here are some of the ways the wind changes:

Oscillations. The wind is almost always shifting back and forth, covering
a range from a few degrees to as much as 40 degrees. This is caused by either
the vertical instability of the air (such as right after a cold front has passed)
or the wind passing over a land mass. If you've ever sailed in a place like the

Charles River in Boston, for example, you know that the wind shifts wildly as it whistles through the skyscraper "canyons."

Persistent shift. Sometimes the wind shifts generally in one direction, due to the passing of a weather system, the geographical influence of the land, or the Coriolis force.

Offshore. A breeze that's blowing from the shore onto the water (such as a high-pressure wind) is generally oscillating. As you get closer to shore, the wind is puffier and shiftier and the water is smoother.

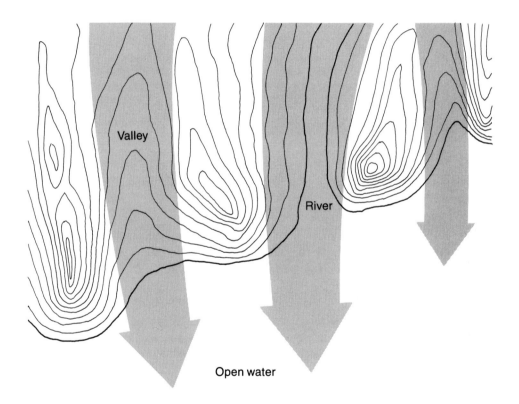

Valley

River

Open water

Offshore breeze—geographic effects.
Whenever you are sailing close to shore, the geography will have a strong influence on wind strength and direction. For example, an offshore breeze will be lighter behind hills or buildings, and stronger where it blows out of bays, rivers, and valleys.

Onshore. A breeze blowing toward shore, such as a sea breeze, is usually quite steady and often persistently shifting. It also brings waves that vary in size according to fetch (the amount of open water to windward) and the strength and duration of the breeze.

Friction effects. Wind near the water surface is slowed and shifted in a counterclockwise direction relative to the wind aloft. When the wind passes over land, it is slowed as much as 30 percent and backed (shifted in a counterclockwise direction) as much as 30 degrees. That's why you'll often get a change in wind direction as you sail toward land.

Geographic effects. Air behaves much like a liquid, reacting to topographical features on land in predictable patterns. Wind will pour down a valley rather than climb over a mountain. By studying the land around your sailing area and observing the wind on the water, you can develop an understanding of the geographic effects on the wind.

CURRENT

Current is the horizontal flow of water relative to the bottom; it can be caused by several different forces. In coastal areas, current is most commonly a result of high and low tides. The gravitational pull of the moon creates a high-tide bulge on the Earth's surface as the moon rotates around the Earth. This results in a constant flow of water as the oceans rise and fall. There are many places in the world where the tide rises and falls as much as 20 or 30 feet.

Weather systems can also cause tidal currents. High-pressure areas push down on the water surface and cause water to flow toward an area of lower atmospheric pressure. The wind also produces currents on large lakes and enclosed bays. A strong breeze blowing from the same direction for several days will push a lot of water into or out of a bay or toward one end of a lake. When the wind subsides, there will be a strong current in the opposite direction as the water returns to its normal position.

Rivers obviously have a strong current flow caused by gravity. Near the mouth of a river, you are likely to experience both tidal conditions and the flow of the river. On the Hudson River, for example, tidal effects are felt many miles north of New York City.

Measuring Current

There are several ways to tell the direction and strength of the current. Before you go out on the water, consult tide tables and current charts for a large-scale picture of what to expect.

When you are out on the water, get in the habit of looking at the movement of the water around buoys or lobster pots to determine the current's direction and approximate strength. To measure current velocity more accurately, drop a floating object into the water next to a fixed object, and check your watch. Take an educated guess at the distance it travels in a set period of time. One hundred feet per minute is roughly equal to one knot of current.

Anchored boats can also give you an indication of the current direction and strength, especially if they are hanging in a direction different than where the wind should be pushing them. When we race out of Annapolis, for example, we keep an eye on the freighters anchored in the middle of Chesapeake Bay. When they swing around in a direction opposite the wind, we know that the current is changing direction out in the deeper channel.

The surface of the water will also give clues about current. The water is relatively smooth when the wind and current are aligned; it is rougher when the current runs against the wind. San Francisco Bay offers one of the more extreme examples of this: On summer afternoons, the sea breeze often builds to more than 20 knots coming right under the Golden Gate Bridge. When the

Measuring current.
An easy way to detect current strength and direction is to look at lobster pots or other buoys anchored to the bottom. Here there is a very strong current of almost 2 knots.

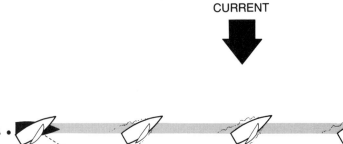

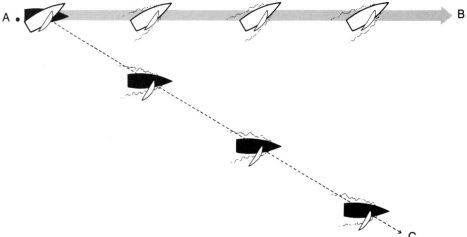

Factoring the effects of current.
When you have a specific destination in mind, you must take current strength and direction
into account. If you steer directly for point B, for example, the current may cause you to end
up at point C. Instead, point your bow into the current so your course made good takes you
directly toward B.

strong currents are ebbing out the bay, there are often violent standing waves that make the area very challenging for small sailboats.

The boundary of two areas with different current is often visible as a disturbed line on the water. Sometimes you can see all sorts of weeds and flotsam along this line. Finally, you can determine current by sensing how your boat and others are moving relative to fixed objects. If you are aiming at a buoy, for example, but you have to keep changing your heading, chances are you are dealing with a crosscurrent.

Effects of Current

Current is very important to racing sailors, who must constantly compensate in order to get around the course as fast as possible. In general, their goal is to sail in areas of more current when it is favorable and less current when it is unfavorable. Starting-line and mark-rounding situations become even trickier (and lots of fun to watch!) when a strong current is running.

Even when cruising or day-sailing, it's important to understand the effects of the current. If you are trying to sail from point A to point B and there is a crosscurrent, you cannot simply aim at point B. The current will carry you well downstream of your destination. Therefore you must sail a course aiming into the current in order to travel in a straight line from A to B. It may even be wise to stay up-current of that line, in case the wind dies.

In light air, it's especially important to keep track of the current. If you're not careful, you may end up so far down-current, you will have a hard time getting home.

11

Safety and Health

One of the best things about sailing is that it's a great way to get in touch with nature. However, sailing is also subject to the tremendous power of nature—power that often runs counter to the safety and health of people on the water. Careful preparation of your boat, equipment, and sailing skills, combined with a healthy respect for the forces of nature, are important to your enjoyment of the sport.

SAFETY CONSIDERATIONS

Sailing safely is largely a matter of thoughtful prevention. If you know the possible dangers and take the necessary precautions, you can save yourself a lot of trouble.

Sun

If there's one thing we've learned from sailing, it's that it is almost impossible to underestimate the effects of the sun while on the water. Not only does the sun hit you from above; it is reflected from the water, sails, and deck. Doctors are only now discovering how widespread skin cancer is. Nearly 10 percent of the population will get this form of cancer during their lives. We are quickly learning that sun is not good for us; in fact, it's very unhealthy.

In our many years on the water, experience has taught us a lot about the effects of the sun. We usually wear a hat while sailing; and you'll almost always find us wearing sunglasses and a strong sun block as well. The most effective hat or visor is one with a dark blue or green underside to reduce glare. Sun-

189

Author David Dellenbaugh using hat, sunglasses, sunscreen, and beard for protection from the sun. Note the leather flaps on the sides of the glasses to protect the eyes from glare.

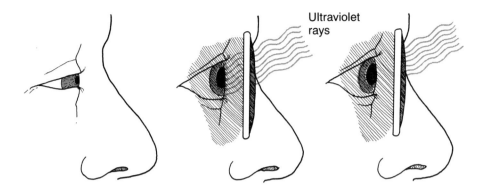

Ultraviolet rays

Sunglasses.
Sunglasses dilate your pupils, so you should make sure that your glasses are the type that will keep harmful rays from getting to your eyes.

glasses must have a very high capacity for blocking the sun's harmful ultraviolet rays, or they may actually dilate your pupils and allow in more harmful rays.

Several top American racing sailors have recently discovered that they have serious cases of sunburn on the cornea, caused by overexposure and underprotection. That's why sunglasses are so important. Unfortunately, effective sunglasses are fairly costly and should be taken care of carefully—there are many pairs at the bottom of the ocean.

With heightened awareness of the harmful effects of the sun, skin care companies are now marketing high SPF (Sun Protection Factor) sun blocks that provide many times your natural protection. Many are reasonably waterproof. In very sunny conditions, we suggest wearing a white long-sleeve T-shirt and light-colored long pants. We don't come back from sailing excursions with much of a tan, but we do feel a lot better knowing that we are preventing long-term sun damage to our skin and eyes.

Heat Stress (Hyperpyrexia)

At the 1986 U.S. Olympic Sports Festival, held in mid-July, we were sailing on Galveston Bay near Houston. Each day on the radio we heard "heat factor warnings" (similar to wind chill factors) which took into account the temperature and the humidity, both of which were near 100. This combination of high temperature, humidity, sun exposure, and exercise can lead to heat stress if the body cannot cool itself sufficiently with evaporating perspiration.

The best way to avoid overheating and sunstroke is to protect yourself from the sun as described above. Try to stay in the shade, minimize your exertion, and drink plenty of fluids. Cold water is most effective and should be drunk regularly *before* you feel thirsty or dehydrated.

If someone on your boat exhibits signs of heat stress (including sluggishness, loss of coordination, and impaired reasoning), take them to a shady place immediately to reduce the body's temperature. Then get medical attention.

Cold and Exposure (Hypothermia)

"Frostbiting" is a type of sailboat racing that started more than 50 years ago along the coast of New England. Seemingly sane sailors venture out on harbor waters every Sunday afternoon all winter long for a series of short races. It's a lot of fun, but it is not without its dangers: hypothermia and overexposure. That's why "crash" boats always stand by very close to the sailors.

The dangers of cold exposure are by no means limited to winter sailing. In fact, extended exposure to water or wind can lead to hypothermia at almost

Frostbiting.
Winter sailboat racing attracts its own hardy breed, who nonetheless dress sensibly to avoid hypothermia and overexposure.

any time of the year. The danger of this condition is that it's hard to detect. Symptoms include paleness, shivering, bluish lips, and a lackadaisical attitude. More advanced symptoms include violent shivering, drowsiness, confusion, and breathing difficulty. The final stages of unconsciousness and irregular heartbeat and breathing are usually fatal.

Immediate medical assistance is a must for exposure victims, and this condition should not be taken lightly. Before help arrives (or if it is not available), protect the victim from further exposure. Begin a slow warm-up process by surrounding the patient with warm bodies; then replace wet clothes with dry clothes or a blanket. Do *not* rub cold areas or give the victim liquids that are warmer than body temperature.

You can minimize your chances of getting hypothermia by wearing appropriate protective clothing and gear (see "Clothing," page 203) and by watching for the early warning signs.

Life Jackets

Dennis Conner, who has won the America's Cup three times, is a great sailor but not a very good swimmer. Dennis loves winning sailboat races, but he doesn't look forward to the traditional "victory plunge" after big victories. The moral is that everyone can enjoy sailing, but some must be especially careful.

If you are not a good swimmer, you should wear a life jacket all the time you are near the water. Even good swimmers are advised to do this. Nearly 85 percent of the people who drown in boating accidents are not wearing life jackets.

Coast Guard regulations require you to carry one appropriately sized PFD (personal flotation device) for each person on board. A number of PFDs on the market today are very comfortable to wear, and we advise wearing one of these vest-type life jackets at all times. You never know when you might fall or get knocked overboard.

There are five types of PFDs, each with different characteristics. The Off-Shore Life Jacket (formerly Type I) will turn an unconscious person face up in the water. This type is obviously the safest. The Near-Shore Life Vest (formerly Type II) has less flotation and will not consistently turn an unconscious person. The Flotation Aid (formerly Type III) distributes its flotation around a person's trunk and performs similarly to the Near-Shore Life Vest. A Throwable Device (formerly Type IV) is a flotable cushion or life ring (required on boats 16 feet or longer), and a Special Use Device (formerly Type V) includes water-skiing belts (which are not considered appropriate PFDs).

Person Overboard!

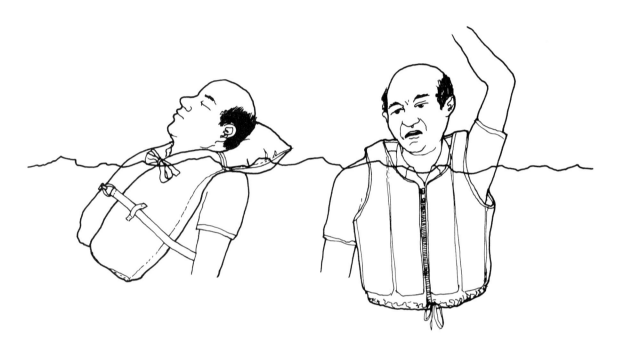

Personal flotation devices.
The safest PFD is the Off-Shore Life Jacket (Type I, not shown), which will turn an unconscious person face up. The Near-Shore Life Vest (Type II, left) and the Flotation Aid (Type III, right) have less flotation and will not consistently turn a person face up, but they are more comfortable and therefore more likely to be worn.

Other Required Safety Equipment

The Coast Guard and state governments have laws that require certain safety gear for boats of various sizes. This includes PFDs, navigation lights, registration numbers, fire extinguishers, distress signals, and so on. Be sure to check with your local Coast Guard Auxiliary or marine police for the complete list of requirements for your type of boat in your state. Even if these items aren't required by law, most of them are good to have anyway.

Electric Power Lines

We grew up racing against a gifted sailor and a great person named Manton Scott. Manton won the Junior National Sailing Championship when he was 17 and then went off to college in Boston. The next thing we heard, he had been electrocuted during a regatta on Cape Cod. While he was pulling his boat through the parking lot on its trailer, the mast came in contact with an electric power line and Manton was killed almost instantly.

Needless to say, this was very sad for us and the rest of the sailing community. Unfortunately, quite a few other sailors have been killed by power lines before and after Manton's death. It's a combination of the lines being situated badly and sailors not being very careful. Over the past several years there has been an active campaign to rid sailing areas, boat ramps, and yacht clubs of these hazards, but the task is not complete and it is still a very real danger. So watch out overhead. If there are power lines near your launching or sailing area, try to have them moved as soon as possible.

Dangers on the Boat

Be sure your equipment is in good shape and properly working. Frayed line or wires should be replaced and all fittings securely attached. Watch out for "meathooks" (broken wire strands that stick out) in wire halyards. Always wear some kind of footwear on small boats, or be willing to risk a severely stubbed toe or cut foot. Watch the boom, especially sailing downwind, when a sudden jibe is possible. And be sure your air tank hatches and plugs are secured to ensure the integrity of the boat's flotation.

Marginal Conditions

It is very important that you know both your own limitations and those of your boat. Pay close attention to weather forecasts and your own observations. If the conditions are extreme, if the wind is blowing offshore, if you are going out alone . . . perhaps you should wait for a better day. If you do decide to go out, stay close to shore and try to get another boat to go along.

Whenever you go sailing, let someone know where you will be going and the expected time of your return. If something breaks or the wind builds or dies, it is good to know that someone will be thinking about you. When you return from sailing, be sure to check in with your contact to let them know you're back.

STORMS

Anticipation and preparation are the key words when discussing storms. By listening to the weather radio and making your own weather observations (see Chapter 10), you should be aware whenever a storm is approaching. Be prudent and don't go sailing if you are unsure of the weather. If conditions change while you are sailing, do everything in your power to get safely into a harbor before the storm hits.

If you are going to have to ride out a storm, there are several precautions you should take. First, all crew members should put on life jackets. Larger boats may have safety harnesses as well. Next, make sure that all hatches, ports, and flotation tank covers are secured, as well as any loose objects that may fly around in a high wind. If you anticipate a storm of short duration, such as a squall, you will want to shorten sail by reefing (reducing the size of the mainsail) or setting smaller storm sails, or take the sails down completely and ride out the storm. To minimize boat speed when riding out the storm, you may want to rig a sea anchor to drag off the stern. This can be a store-bought model, but anything creating a lot of drag will suffice.

If you will be sailing for extended periods offshore, you should familiarize yourself with more extensive storm procedures found in valuable resources such as *The Annapolis Book of Seamanship* (see the Bibliography).

CAPSIZE!

While most keelboats will not tip over because of the righting action of their heavy keels, centerboard boats are subject to capsize. Our first advice is to sail a "self-rescuing" boat—one that is easy to right in case you do capsize. A self-rescuing boat has large flotation tanks so it will float high in the water when capsized and will come up with little water in the cockpit when righted. Some boats have a self-draining cockpit that gets rid of any water left in the bilge once you start sailing again. Otherwise you will need a bucket or bailer (tied to the boat so it doesn't float away or sink) to bail out the remaining water manually.

If you're sailing in windy conditions, wear your life jacket. If you do capsize, first make sure that everyone is all right and that no one is trapped in the boat, caught under the sails, or tangled in sheets or rigging. The next most important rule is to *stay with the boat.* Don't try to swim for land or to recover objects floating away from the boat. Once you start swimming, you will get tired and cold much sooner than you think. It is also easier for rescuers to see a capsized hull than a person swimming.

Righting the Boat

When the boat capsizes, try to prevent it from turning "turtle," or upside down. It is far more difficult to right a turtled boat than one lying on its side. The best way to do this is to hop over the rail quickly and stand on the centerboard.

Once everyone is o.k. and settled down, you can begin to right the boat. Make sure the sheets and boom vang are eased, so the sails won't fill with wind again and pull you back over. One crew member should hold on to the centerboard, initially to prevent the boat from turtling, then to right the boat. Pull down on the centerboard, or if you are on the centerboard, pull down on the rail, and your weight will slowly right the boat. If you need more leverage, pull on the jib sheet over the top of the boat.

While this is happening, the other crew is in the water, on the cockpit side of the boat, holding the mast up by the gooseneck. As the boat begins to right, the crew member by the cockpit holds on to a hiking strap, traveler bar, or anything secure inside the cockpit and is literally scooped into the boat. This person has been saved the struggle of climbing into the boat and can now assist the others getting in.

This technique works well when you capsize with the mast pointing away from the wind. When your boat tips over to windward, however, there is a problem: the wind will catch the underside of the sails as they rise out of the water and quickly flip the boat over to leeward, right on top of you. To prevent this, push the bow around so that the boat is pointing into the wind. A more advanced technique is to use the "scoop" method described above. The crew member who gets scooped into the boat must balance the boat and prevent it from capsizing to leeward.

In shallow water, you can run into the problem of the mast getting stuck

Righting a Capsized Boat: The Less Preferred Method

When you capsize, climb quickly onto the centerboard to keep the boat from turning "turtle" (upside down). Make sure that all crew members are wearing life jackets (A).

A

Use your body weight on the centerboard to right the boat (B, C).

B

C

The problem with having both crew members on the same side of the boat is that there is no one to steady the side that comes out of the water. Result: the boat may flip over on top of you.

D

Righting a Capsized Boat:
The Scoop Method (Preferred)

A   B

The best way to right your boat is to use the "scoop" method. One crew member puts his weight on the centerboard while the other remains in the water, holding on to something secure in the cockpit (A, B).

As the boat comes upright, the crew on the centerboard goes back into the water, and the other crew is "scooped" right into the cockpit (E, F).

E   F

C

D

With one crew member on the centerboard, the boat begins to come upright (C, D).

The crew who is in the cockpit can now steady the boat and keep it from capsizing again. He also helps the other crew member get back in the boat (G).

G

in the mud, with the wind and waves pushing it farther in. In this case you may have to push the bow around so that the mast is pointing to windward. Now the wind and waves will help unstick the mast.

A turtled boat is difficult to right because you have less leverage and a longer way to go. It will be even more difficult if the centerboard slides back into the hull, so try to keep it sticking up. Stand on the windward rail and use either the centerboard or the leeward jib sheet, brought over the boat, to slowly right the boat.

PERSON OVERBOARD

When sailing offshore, one of the biggest fears of any crew member is falling overboard or losing another person overboard. Unless you are a skilled sailor and disciplined at man-overboard procedure, finding someone and getting them back on board can be a difficult and terrifying experience.

The Sailing Foundation of Seattle and the Naval Academy Sailing Squadron recently conducted extensive trials on man-overboard recovery and found that a method called the "Quick-stop" minimizes the separation distance and recovery time. The USYRU (U.S. Yacht Racing Union) Safety-at-Sea Committee has published a report on these results. Anyone who is sailing offshore or in larger boats should take the time to read and practice the various search-and-recovery procedures.

Fortunately, falling off a smaller boat is not quite so serious. Day sailers are usually not too far from land, they don't sail as fast, they sail in calmer waters, and they don't have as much freeboard (height of the deck above the water), so it's easier to get someone out of the water. However, falling overboard is still a danger, and every sailor should know how to handle this situation. This includes all crew members, in case the knowledgeable boat owner/skipper falls over.

When someone goes overboard, head up immediately and let the sails luff, to slow your boat. Keep an eye on the person in the water to make sure they are o.k. Then head away on a beam reach, tack back to a beam reach, and aim just to leeward of the person in the water. Adjusting speed with the sails, head up just to leeward of the person and slow the boat to a stop. Then help the person over the windward side or transom, being sure to balance their weight with your own.

It's a great idea to practice this maneuver using a flotation cushion. When the rest of the people on your boat aren't looking, throw a cushion over the side and yell, "Man overboard." Then see what happens. By practicing this way, you'll be in good shape if you ever have to deal with the real thing.

Man Overboard!

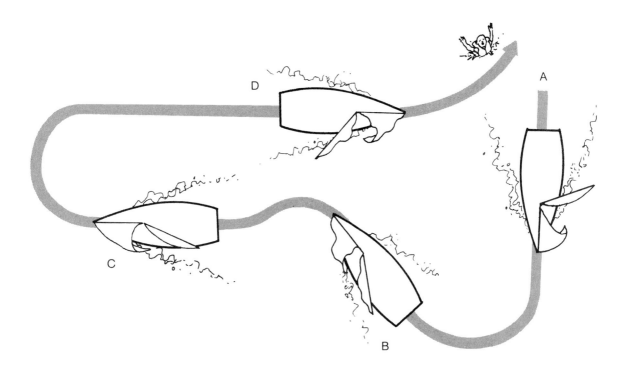

If a person falls overboard (A), head up and let the sails luff to slow the boat (B). Head away on a beam reach (C), tack back to a beam reach (D), and aim just to leeward of the person overboard. By adjusting speed with the sails, you should be able to stop to leeward and alongside the person. Throughout the procedure, keep the overboard person in your sight.

SEASICKNESS

Getting seasick is a good way to ruin a nice day on the water. If you are prone to seasickness, don't worry—you're not alone. Some of the very best and most experienced sailors get sick in certain conditions. I'm a good example. The last time I did the Bermuda Race, we got into some mixed-up waves during the first night, when we were out of sight of land, and I got very sick. Fortunately I recovered fairly quickly, but I can tell you it's not a fun experience.

There are several things you can do to prevent, or minimize, seasickness:

• If you go out on a windy day, sail mainly in protected areas, where the water is smoother.

• If you're on a boat with a cabin, stay on deck and don't go down below (don't even look down below).

• Keep your eyes focused on something distant and unmoving, like the shoreline or horizon.

• Take a turn at the helm. Steering is often the best way to stave off seasickness.

• Use a motion-sickness medication such as standard over-the-counter pills, Transderm Scop (a prescription adhesive patch you wear on the skin behind your ear), or a prescription pill (there are some good drugs that NASA developed for the astronauts). With any of these, be sure to take them well before you get into rough seas, so you won't get sick before the drug takes effect. Also, be sure you read the label on every medication, since some have undesirable side effects.

GETTING IN SHAPE

Sailing, like other sports, makes physical demands on your body, especially if you exert yourself in an activity like hiking out, pumping the sheets, or grinding winches. People who spend a lot of time racing small boats have to spend just as much time getting their bodies into shape as any other athlete.

If you're a casual sailor, the physical aspects usually aren't so demanding (and that's why you will enjoy this sport for many years to come). Still, there are ways to train for sailing and to minimize the chance of injury.

Strength. In windy weather, it's helpful to have good arm and leg strength for trimming and hiking. During the 1987 America's Cup trials in Australia, our crew used special exercise machines that simulated the motion and resistance of grinding winches to build up our arm strength.

Endurance. Aerobic exercise such as swimming, running, or bicycling helps increase your endurance by improving oxygen delivery to exercising muscles.

Flexibility. The best way to prevent sore or pulled muscles is to increase their flexibility by stretching. You should warm up your muscles before sailing and cool them down afterward with a complete stretching routine.

Nutrition

Like good physical conditioning, every athlete needs good nutrition. Especially important for sailors is the intake of liquids while sailing—it's very easy to get dehydrated in the heat and sun. A rule of thumb is to drink at least one pint of liquid every hour. The best liquid you can drink is water. We usually freeze water in bicycle squirt bottles the night before going sailing. These melt and stay cold while sailing, and they're easy to squirt in your mouth or onto your salty face or sunglasses.

CLOTHING

Dressing for a day on the water usually is not as easy as getting ready for a tennis match or a golf game, because sailors are exposed to a wide variety of weather. No matter where you are, the combination of water and wind can turn even the hottest day into a chilling experience. And unless you're on a boat with a cabin, there's nowhere to go to get out of the elements.

There are several qualities to look for in sailing clothing. It should be: (1) lightweight and nonrestrictive, so you can move around easily; (2) waterproof, so you're protected from the spray, but also breatheable, so you won't get all sweaty inside; and (3) warm, so you won't freeze.

Sailing gear has improved a lot during recent years, but it has also gotten quite expensive. The amount that you'll want to invest in specialty clothing is probably proportional to the amount of sailing you're planning to do during the next couple of years. Here are some of the items you may want to consider:

Footwear	Boating shoes Rubber sailing boots	**Head wear**	Visor or baseball hat Wool watch cap
Inside layers	Polypropylene long underwear	**Gloves**	Leather sailing gloves Warmer gloves
Foul-weather gear	Two-piece suit One-piece suit	**Specialty**	Wet suit Dry suit

Clothing

Footwear.

There are many types of footwear that work for small-boat sailing. If you wear a sneaker, try to get a boating version with special nonskid soles (left). For better protection, try a sailing boot. The lace-up hiking boot (center) offers a snug fit, excellent traction, reinforcement for hiking, and protection from water. For even drier and warmer feet, you could try a full sea boot (right). We don't recommend these for small boats, however, because they are too heavy and bulky. They're also potentially dangerous if you capsize because they can fill up with water.

Foul-weather gear.

The standard wet gear for small-boat sailors is a one-piece foul-weather suit. This type of suit, made from a light waterproof material, offers protection from spray and lets you move around easily.

Two-piece foul-weather gear.
The two-piece foul-weather suit is more waterproof than a one-piece suit, but it is also heavier and bulkier. It is a good all-around compromise if you will be sailing on big boats as well as small boats.

Layering.
If you want to keep warm while sailing, go with the layered approach. The layer closest to your skin should be polypropylene or some other synthetic that "wicks" moisture away from your skin.

Wet suits and dry suits.
A wet suit (left) offers good warmth and protection if you don't mind a layer of water between your skin and the suit. A dry suit (right) has seals around its neck, wrists, and ankles, so you will stay warm and dry even if you fall overboard. Both suits are expensive, so they should be considered only by serious sailors or those who sail a lot in cold air or water.

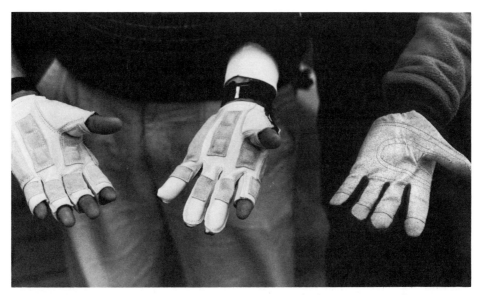

Sailing gloves.
These are a great idea for anyone with untoughened hands, especially when sailing on a windy day. You can choose from a wide variety of styles ranging from cut-offs (left), to partial cut-offs (center), to full-fingered (right), depending on how much warmth and protection you desire.

Hats.
There are many ways to keep rain, spray, and cold air off your head, and here are a few. Remember that without a hat, you lose a great deal of body heat through your head.

12

Beginning to Race

Racing sailboats is a mental chess game, and a challenge that is hard to turn down. It's also a way to measure your own abilities and to see how much you have learned. Racing will definitely improve your sailing skills. Sooner or later anyone who is really keen about the sport will want to get beside another boat and give it his best.

Since the schooner *America* sailed around the Isle of Wight and won the Hundred Guineas Cup in 1851, competitive sailing has grown by leaps and bounds. The 1987 America's Cup, for example, was watched by millions of viewers all over the world. And it is estimated that nearly half a million people currently race sailboats in the United States alone.

The sport of yacht racing is organized worldwide by a body called the International Yacht Racing Union (IYRU). Each country has its own sailing authority as well. In the U.S., for example, the U.S. Yacht Racing Union (USYRU) oversees most of the racing that takes place.

TYPES OF RACING

Depending on the type of boat you sail and where you live, there are a number of different ways that boats compete against each other.

One-Design

Almost all racing in smaller boats is what's called "one-design," and it takes place at yacht clubs and other sailing centers. In this type of racing, all the boats are basically the same, so the first one across the finish line is the winner. Each

209

One of the surest ways to develop your sailing skills is to race.

class has rules to control the equality of the boats. The fun and challenge of one-design racing is that winning requires skill, not more money or a fancier design.

Handicap

There are several different handicap systems for racing boats of various sizes and designs. Boats are given ratings determined by measurements of hull and sails, by their predicted speed, or by past performance. A faster-rated boat gives a specific amount of time per mile to a slower boat. The time each boat takes to sail the course is recorded, and the corrected time is calculated by adding the time allowances to determine an overall winner. In handicap racing, the last boat across the finish line might win the race.

Various handicap systems have been developed to best meet the needs of different types of sailboats, including grand prix ocean racers, older racing boats, cruising/family boats, and one-design boats of different classes. The Portsmouth Handicap System, for example, allows different one-designs to race against each other and is the only system you'd ever use for a small boat.

THE TYPICAL RACE

Every race and series is governed by the IYRU racing rules, by class rules (if applicable), and by written sailing instructions that are drawn up specially for the event. The IYRU rules describe the signals and procedures that the race committee will use to run the races. The class rules specify any measurement requirements and may require certain safety equipment to be carried. The sailing instructions give you the specifics of the race or series, including the schedule of events and races, the racing area, the course configuration, what the marks look like, time limits, safety considerations, and so on. Often at the beginning of a regatta there will be a "skippers' meeting" to provide additional information and answer questions.

Before the start, the race committee will mark the course and set up a starting line, usually between a flag on their boat and a buoy. Visual and sound signals are used to count down the time to the start, beginning with a warning signal (usually 10 minutes before the start), followed by the preparatory signal (5 minutes to the start), and then the starting signal.

The typical small-boat course goes around a series of buoys, called marks, the first of which is directly upwind from the starting line. This is called the

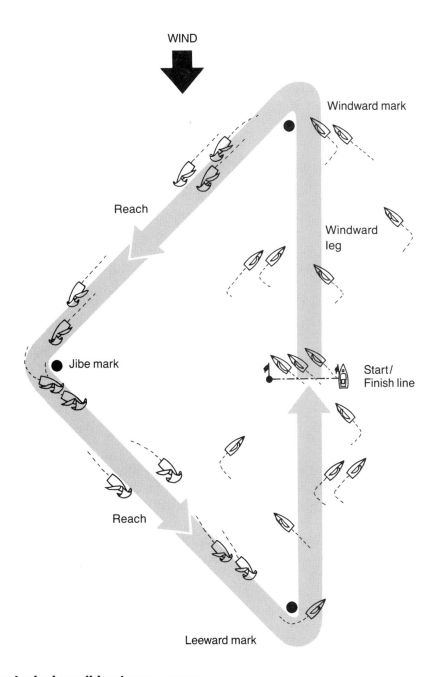

WIND

Windward mark

Reach

Windward leg

Jibe mark

Start/
Finish line

Reach

Leeward mark

The typical small-boat race course
is a triangle that starts and finishes with the boats sailing to windward.

windward mark, and it forces the competitors to start to windward and tack up the first leg, creating close racing. Depending on the type of course, the next mark will be either a jibe mark or a leeward mark. If you go to the jibe mark, you will reach out to the mark, jibe around it, then reach down to the leeward mark. If you go straight to the leeward mark from the windward mark, you will bear off onto a run. After the leeward mark, you will beat back to windward.

INGREDIENTS OF SUCCESS

In order to be successful at racing, a sailor must have a wide range of skills. Consider the America's Cup, for example. In a serious campaign, the actual sailing is only a small part of the program, perhaps as little as 10 to 20 percent. The rest is spent raising money, designing and building the boat, getting in shape, repairing the boat, and so on. Many people have suggested that Dennis Conner is not the world's best helmsman; however, he is right up there when it comes to planning and executing America's Cup campaigns.

There are five areas where the sailor must concentrate in order to improve her or his racing performance: preparation, boat handling, boat speed, strategy, and tactics.

Preparation

Preparation includes everything you must do before the race committee shoots the first gun. Among the most important elements of preparation is making sure your boat will hold together. We can't count the number of times we've seen a race lost because of a breakdown. All the blocks, lines, cotter pins, and other equipment should be checked to ensure that they are in good working order. Regular maintenance, cleaning, and replacement of worn parts is essential.

Careful preparation of the boat's underwater surfaces is also very important. The hull, centerboard, and rudder should be clean and smooth. Fill in nicks and gouges to minimize disturbances in the water flow.

Organization is integral in sailboat racing. How will we get the boat there? Do we have all the pieces? Spare parts? Tools? When do we have to be ready to sail? Where will we stay? Who's in charge of the food? Do we have our life jackets? Sails? Paddle? We use several checklists to make sure we don't forget anything. This lets us concentrate more on the actual racing.

Soling Checklist
Bring on the Boat

Mainsails:	Heavy air	Protest flag ("B")
	Light air	Screwdriver
Jibs:	Heavy air	Pliers
	Light air	Spare line
Spinnakers:	Runner	Spare blocks
	Reacher	Spare shackles, pins, etc.
	Mini	Rigging knife
		Pencils
Spinnaker Pole		Marking pen
		Current stick
Safety:	Life jackets	Telltales
	Buckets (3)	Tape
	Pump	
	Sponge	Sunglasses
	Anchor and	Hats
	anchor line	Sunscreen
	Paddle	
		Water bottles
Hiking harnesses		Food
		Sailing instructions
		Chart of the racing area

During his recent Olympic campaign in the Soling class with Don Cohan, Brad Dellenbaugh used this checklist to make sure that no important items were left on shore.

Boat Handling

Boat handling refers to how the skipper and crew handle their boat in maneuvers like tacks, jibes, mark roundings, and spinnaker work. Large gains (and losses) can be made during these maneuvers, and again, practice is the key.

The various boat-handling maneuvers should become second nature so that you can concentrate on the race around you. Imagine rounding the windward mark in first place, with the rest of the fleet right on your heels. *Pop!* Your crew expertly sets the spinnaker, it fills, and off you go on a plane, leaving the fleet in your wake to battle for second. Without the ability to execute this perfect set, you would have a lot of company for the remainder of the race.

Crew training should be a big part of pre-race preparation, since it is usually too hectic in the middle of a race to calmly discuss the best way to take down the spinnaker. Arrange for practice sessions when you can concentrate on practicing new maneuvers and smoothing out any boat-handling areas that have given you trouble in recent races.

Boat Speed

As you get more racing experience, you may notice that the top sailors not only get off to good starts and demonstrate good boat handling, they are also just plain *fast*. This boat speed comes from a combination of factors including rig tuning, sail trim, steering technique, and boat preparation.

Rig tuning refers to the position of your mast and the tension of the shrouds and backstay. These factors control mast bend and, in turn, affect the shape and efficiency of the sails. Subtle changes in sail trim controls—sheets, leads, outhaul, cunningham, vang—will allow your sails to take advantage of the conditions.

The ability to steer a boat well, especially in wavy or choppy conditions, is one of the secrets to good speed—and also takes much practice. Knowing when and how much to head up or off to avoid a wave, or how to trim the sails when you can't avoid a wave, is a fine art. Other factors contributing to boat speed include the fairness (smoothness) of the hull and foils (no weeds or barnacles here!), minimizing windage (objects that create wind friction) especially in the rigging, and sailing in clear, undisturbed air (away from other boats).

Don't worry if this seems complicated at first. You can always get general guidelines for tuning your rig and trimming your sails from class members, sailmakers, or magazine articles. As you become more familiar with your boat and are more competitive in your racing, you can begin to experiment with speed variables on your own.

Strategy

Strategy is your plan for getting around the race course as fast as possible. When formulating a strategy, you have to consider wind, current, and sea conditions. For example, you want to figure out if there is a pattern in the wind. Is it shifting back and forth (oscillating) or is it gradually shifting in one direction (persistent)? Where is the most wind? What is the weather (and wind) forecast?

Current can also play an important role. Sailing in the Southern Ocean Racing Conference off the east coast of Florida, it can often be advantageous to sail a much longer course to get out to the Gulf Stream, which may push you northward at up to 4 knots! Knowing the direction and strength of the current on all parts of the course is valuable.

Sea conditions are often an overlooked aspect of strategy. Does one side of the course have smoother water? Does rougher water indicate more favorable current, a longer fetch (open water to windward) for the seas to build up, or shallower water? Part of your preparation before a race is to accumulate this information so you will have a game plan to follow once the race has begun.

Tactics

Tactics are the tools you possess for executing your strategy in a fleet of boats. The object is not to let other boats get in the way of your plan. Some of the questions you must deal with continually are: How do you position yourself relative to the other boats? Can you control where your closest competitors go or prevent them from getting toward the favored side? How can you minimize your risks? What rules take effect when boats come together?

There are books and articles galore on tactics, but the best learning experience is lots of racing and observation. You will gradually build up your own repertoire of tactical moves for each situation that arises.

RULES OF THUMB FOR RACING

No matter what kind of racing you do, there are a few general rules of thumb that apply.

Get out to the starting area early, at least an hour before the start if possible. Use your time to:

- accumulate information on the wind, current, and sea conditions;
- check on your sail trim and tuning, possibly by sailing upwind with another boat;
- check on the course, locating the marks if possible;
- make sure everyone knows their assignments on the boat;
- warm up with some tacks and jibes; and
- figure out which end of the starting line is favored.

At the starting gun, you should be on the line, moving with clear air. This is the most important thing, especially when you are just starting to race.

Sail in clear air. In order to sail at full speed, your wind must be undisturbed by other boats. Every boat has a wind shadow of "bad air" that extends several boat lengths to leeward and astern. If you are in bad air, you need to get clear by tacking or reaching off slightly.

Stay away from the lay lines. The lay lines are the imaginary lines that lead to the windward mark on port and starboard tacks. Don't get to either lay line too early, because if you sail beyond the lay line, you have "overstood" the mark and wasted distance. Also, you will lose distance to the competition if the wind shifts in either direction. And if you are on the lay line when another boat tacks on your air, you'll have to sail all the way to the mark in bad air.

Stick to the rhumb lines. The rhumb line is the straight-line course between two marks. On a reach or run, the rhumb line is the shortest distance between two marks, and it is fastest to follow this course whenever possible.

Cover when you're ahead. When you want to protect your lead, position your boat so you are between your competition and the next mark. This minimizes their chances of catching you.

Find the upwind groove. You'll know when your boat is going fast upwind because it will feel right. The boat seems balanced and is easy to steer, usually with a slight weather helm. This is called being "in the groove."

Some Rules of Thumb for Racing

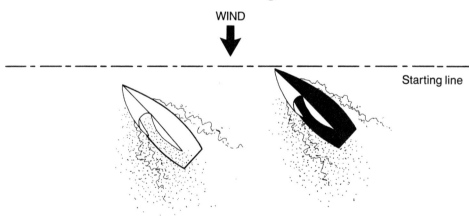

WIND

Starting line

At the starting gun, be on the line, moving with clear air.
It's not easy to be on the line at the gun, but you should be as close as possible, with good boat speed, and your air clear of other boats.

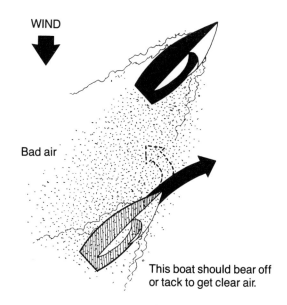

Sail in clear air.

Every boat casts a "wind shadow" of disturbed air that extends several boat lengths to leeward. In order to sail fast, you must avoid these areas of bad air.

WIND

Bad air

This boat should bear off or tack to get clear air.

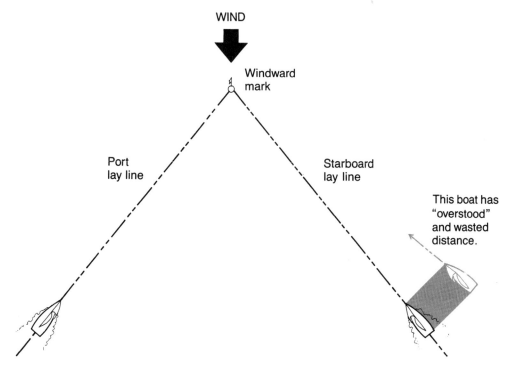

WIND

Windward mark

Port lay line

Starboard lay line

This boat has "overstood" and wasted distance.

Stay away from the lay lines.

The lay lines are the imaginary lines that lead to the windward mark on starboard and port tack. When racing, it is usually a good idea to stay away from the lay lines until you are close to the windward mark.

Next mark

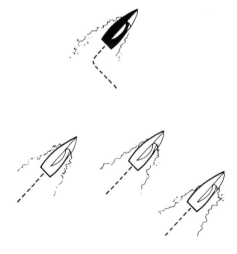

Cover when you are ahead.
A basic racing principle is to
"cover" when ahead—that is,
stay between the next mark and
the boats behind you. This will
maximize your chance of staying
ahead of them.

Avoid collisions. Even when you have the right of way, one of the basic concepts of racing is to avoid collisions. Too much damage can be done, and it will ruin the fun for all involved. Besides, getting tangled up with other boats will slow you down.

Watch the good guys. No matter what else you do, keep an eye on the experienced sailors. This will teach you more than anything else. If possible, get a crewing job with a good sailor. This is the best way to learn quickly.

Keep a notebook. After every race, write down what you learned about boat handling, tactics, wind shifts, tuning, and sail trim. Make notes of things you did well and things you need to work on, and review these with your crew.

CRITICAL PARTS OF THE RACE

Certain parts of most races require a little extra concentration.

Finding the line. At the starting signal, you want to be at the starting line, but not over it. If you are over the line early, you must return behind the line while staying clear of the other boats.

Use a range to determine how close you are to the line: Get a line sight (or "range") before the start by lining up both ends of the starting line with an object on shore. When you are in the middle of the line, one end of the line and your range will line up.

Decide on the best starting position. Unless the starting line is set exactly perpendicular to the wind, one end will be farther upwind ("favored") and therefore will give a boat starting at that end an advantage. However, if you see a pack of boats converging on the favored end, start down the line a little to avoid the traffic jam—you want to have clear air when you start. Be sure that your starting position helps you follow your race strategy; if you saw more wind on the right side of the course, for example, don't start at the left end of the line.

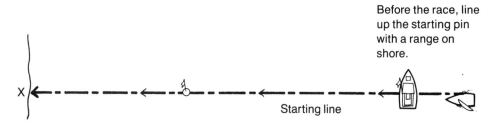

Before the race, line up the starting pin with a range on shore.

Starting line

Range on shore

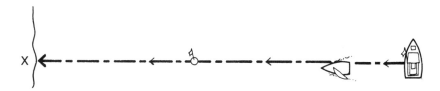

Finding the line.
When you're in the middle of the starting line, it's hard to know how close you are to the line. To solve the problem before the race, line up the two ends of the line with a range on shore (top). Then, as you approach the start, you can use the pin end and your range to find the line (bottom).

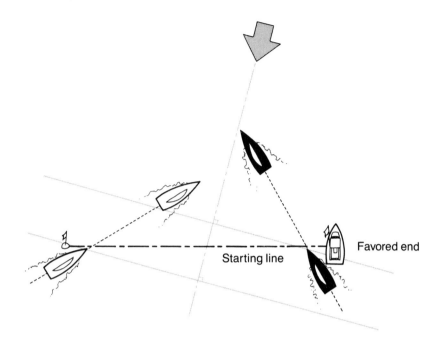

Starting line

Favored end

The favored end
of the starting line is the one that's more upwind. A boat that starts at the favored end will cross ahead of a boat starting at the other end.

Windward Legs

Follow the strategy that you formulated before the start. Stay in clear air and work on boat speed. Use other boats as guides for speed and wind shifts. It seldom pays to sail way out to one side of the course.

Leeward Legs

Keep your air clear of the wind shadows from the boats just behind you. Pick a sailing angle that maximizes your velocity made good toward the mark— sometimes you can gain by heading up slightly away from the mark, as long as this increases your speed enough to make up for the extra distance sailed. Toward the end of the leg, position your boat so you will have the inside position as you prepare to round the leeward mark.

Mark Roundings

Going around a mark is usually exciting because all the boats come together and try to jam into the same little spot. Boat-handling skills and knowledge of the rules are very important here. In general, you should always round the mark close enough so you can reach out and touch it (but of course you don't want to hit it).

Rounding a mark is one of the more exciting and demanding aspects of racing.

Finishing

Determine the favored end. Unless the finish line is exactly perpendicular to the wind, you should always finish at one end. When finishing upwind, the end that is farther downwind is favored. When finishing downwind, the end that is farther upwind is favored.

"Shoot" the line. In close finishes, the quickest way to finish is to go head to wind ("shoot") just before you reach the line, so you cross it on a perpendicular heading with full momentum.

SPORTSMANSHIP AND RULES

There's one more important area that you should understand before you go out there and start racing. This has to do with the racing rules. The yacht racing rules have developed over the years not only to help avoid collisions, but also to make racing fair. Like any sport, rules are necessary to establish a common ground of understanding and keep the "game" under control. Imagine football without referees!

Sailing is one of the few sports where competitors themselves enforce the rules, so whenever you feel that a rule has been violated, your response should be to protest. If the offending boat does not accept a penalty, then the matter is presented to a protest committee after the race is done. This is a bit like a court hearing, with both sides presenting their case and the protest committee (or jury) applying the appropriate "laws."

The basic racing rules are fairly easy to understand. Whenever two boats converge on the race course, they are related in one of four ways, and must move accordingly:

1. *On opposite tacks:* the boat on port tack must keep clear of the boat on starboard tack.

2. *On the same tack—overlapped:* the windward boat must keep clear of the leeward boat.

3. *On the same tack—not overlapped:* the boat that is clear astern must keep clear of the boat that is clear ahead.

4. *One or both boats changing tacks or jibes:* the boat that is tacking or jibing must stay clear of the boat on a tack.

These basic rules will handle most simple situations between two boats. Remember that the right-of-way boat must hold her course so other boats can keep clear. When you are ready for more complicated rules, get a copy of the

Some Basic Rules of Racing

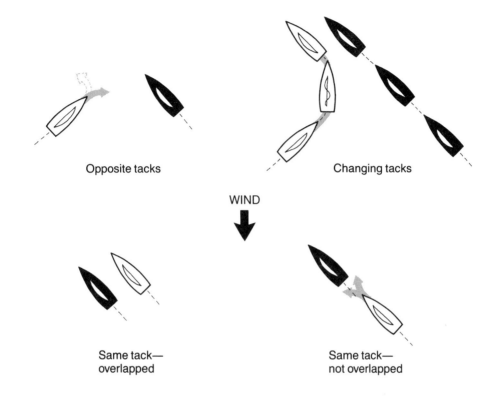

Opposite tacks

Changing tacks

WIND

Same tack—
overlapped

Same tack—
not overlapped

When two boats converge on the race course, they are always related in one of four ways, as shown here. In each case, the rules of racing say that the white boat must keep clear of the black boat.

IYRU rulebook. Do everything possible to increase your understanding of the rules—read books and articles, watch a rules videotape, and ask other sailors or judges about specific incidents. It is in everyone's best interest that sailors educate themselves to keep the sport fair and fun.

This chapter has obviously covered only the fundamentals of what goes into successful sailboat racing. If you find this exciting and challenging, you'll want to get hold of some of the many other, more detailed instructional resources. And you'll want to get a lot of on-the-water experience.

13

Getting More Involved in the Sport

So you've been bitten by the bug. You went out sailing recently and had a great time. Then you bought this book and read it cover to cover. Now you're ready to get more involved in the sport. What can you do?

Unlike most other recreational activities, sailing is a limited-access sport. This unfortunate situation is a result of several factors. The most obvious is that you need a boat to go sailing. If you've looked into buying, you know the cost can be prohibitive. It is possible to buy a sailboard for as little as $500, but even the most inexpensive day sailer will run you at least $2,000. And if you want a boat for overnight cruising, you're looking at a minimum of $15,000.

A second sailing requirement is, of course, water. Even if you're fortunate enough to live near the ocean or a lake, you still must find access to this precious resource. Most waterfront property is expensive and private nowadays, which makes it difficult to find places to launch or moor a boat. Many areas have yacht clubs with good facilities, but most of these are also very expensive to join, especially for someone just getting into the sport.

SAILING OPPORTUNITIES

Fortunately, there are now a number of ways for people to get involved in sailing. Thanks to the America's Cup and increased media attention on the sport, more people are coming into sailing than ever before. This means that the opportunities are much greater than they have ever been.

Probably the best way to try out the sport is to go out with a friend who has a boat. More people own boats now than ever, so there's a good chance that someone you know has their own sailboat. Going with a friend will give you

225

Many people are fortunate to be part of college sailing programs (shown here). If you take up the sport after school, however, community sailing programs can provide splendid opportunities to get more involved in the sport.

the opportunity to try out the sport without any financial commitment. It's also a great way to learn, since most sailors love to share their knowledge and enthusiasm about the sport.

Of course you don't want to impose on friends—but be aware that many sailboat owners are often looking for crew, especially if they do any racing. Your eagerness to learn and willingness to make a commitment to sail with them may make you a welcome addition to their crew.

Community Sailing

If your friends aren't into sailing, don't despair. There are many other ways to get out on the water. One of these is community sailing centers. A number of cities (such as Boston, Milwaukee, and Seattle) now have public sailing programs that give thousands of people a chance to go sailing each year for a small price. With these programs you typically pay an annual membership fee, which entitles you to use the boats as often as you wish. Many centers also offer sailing classes and other group activities.

Sailing Schools

If you want a more focused learning experience, try a sailing school—there are currently more than 200 in the United States. Most of these use small centerboard boats or keelboats for instruction, and offer courses that last from a few hours to a week. They teach everything from basic seamanship to boat handling and beginning racing. The best thing about sailing schools is that they will quickly improve your sailing skills and thereby make sailing more fun. They'll also introduce you to other people in your area who are enthusiastic about the sport, and will likely open up sailing opportunities.

Chartering

Another way to get on the water is by chartering. The typical charter involves a large, roomy cruising boat somewhere in the Caribbean. It's possible, however, to charter almost any kind of boat anywhere around the world. If you don't have much sailing experience, you will have to get what's called a "crewed" charter, where a captain comes along to manage the boat. Sometimes it's possible to get a captain who will also function as an instructor, so you can charter and learn at the same time. Eventually you may be able to "bareboat" charter, or take the boat by yourself.

Although you can find pleasurable charter opportunities closer to home, perhaps the ultimate charter is a roomy cruising boat on the Caribbean.

BUYING A BOAT

If you really get hooked on sailing, sooner or later you will want to buy. There's nothing quite like having your own boat. It gives you the freedom to go sailing whenever and wherever you want. And you have the "opportunity" to spend many hours learning the skills of boat maintenance.

When you're in the market for a boat, it's not always so easy to find out what's available. Boat shows are one good source of information, but they tend to feature bigger boats. To find out more about the small-boat arena, talk to your local boat dealers as well as all your sailing friends. Also, some of the national sailing magazines publish good annual issues listing all the boats available on the market.

Here are some of the factors you should consider (in rough order of their importance) when buying a boat:

Size. Will you be sailing this boat by yourself? Can your kids handle it? Or do you want a boat that can accommodate you and three of your best friends? In general, smaller is better (especially when you're starting) because it's less expensive and easier to launch, sail, and store. Smaller boats are also more sensitive to steering and weight placement, which is a plus if you're keen on learning the finer points of sailing.

Safety. Perhaps the most important quality in a boat is the ability to self-right. In other words, when a boat capsizes, can the crew easily right it and continue sailing? The last thing you want is to capsize and not be able to get your boat back up. What you should look for is a small self-draining cockpit and large, tightly sealed flotation tanks. Sunfish and Lasers, for example, are simple to get back up when you turn them over because they have small cockpits and large waterproof tank areas.

Ease of transport and rigging. Sailing should be easy and enjoyable. If you have to spend an hour or two getting your boat ready each time you go out, that's not too much fun. Unless you have a mooring, a priority in buying a boat should be ease of rigging and launching. Boats that are light enough to put on top of your car, for example, are usually the most hassle-free.

Cost. Unfortunately, cost is a factor in almost any boat-buying decision. There are quite a few used boats on the market these days, and this is often where you can find the best value. Fiberglass construction will give you better durability and easier maintenance than wood.

Performance. Try not to base your buying decision solely on economics. The least expensive boat probably won't keep you happy for too long—chances are you will soon be ready for a bigger challenge. A more "performance-oriented" boat often gives you better value in the long run. This type of boat is light, fast, and usually a bit tippy, but it gives you more challenges and learning opportunities. If performance appeals to you, consider getting a boat with a spinnaker (and possibly a trapeze) that will plane easily.

Outboard. If you sail in an area with light wind, or if you have to travel a long way out of a harbor or river to get to your sailing area, you might want to consider having an outboard motor. This will save you time and, possibly, a lot of paddling. Many small boats are not designed to carry an outboard on the transom, so make sure you check this out.

Cruising comforts. If you'd like the option to cruise overnight, get a boat with a cabin, a cooler, and some type of head (toilet). There are quite a few small cruising boats that can be trailered and also make good learning boats.

Racing potential. If you would like to get into racing, this should be a major consideration when buying a boat. Almost all small sailing boats race as one-design classes, so research your local area to see what fleets are racing there already. Often the members of these fleets can arrange for you to go sailing in their class, and can help you with buying information. If there are several different classes in your area, check to see which has the strongest national organization.

LEARNING MORE

Once you've found a way to get out on the water, it probably won't be long before you start looking for new ways to learn more. There are a large number of books on sailing (see the Bibliography), and there are also a number of excellent periodicals. If you are sailing in a one-design class, be sure to join the class association so you will get their newsletter. This publication will contain all sorts of useful information about your boat and class.

Another good way to learn is simply to go out and practice. Whether you are trying to learn how to set a spinnaker or drop an anchor, there's nothing quite like trying it a few times. As they say, practice makes perfect. If you're inclined toward racing, a great place to practice is in a hands-on sailing seminar. This type of on-the-water instruction is typically sponsored by a yacht club, one-design class, or sailing association. Contact the U.S. Yacht Racing Union for more information on sailing instruction. One final place to look for instruction is the marine industry. Some sailmakers, for example, offer instructional weekend seminars during the winter.

No matter what your level of sailing ability, there is always a way for you

Sailing is fun at any level, and as even the most seasoned sailor will tell you, there is always something new to learn.

to take the next step and get more involved in the sport. It's been a little tough to do this in the past, due to limited access and the expense of participation. But now that sailing is receiving much more attention from the media and from corporate sponsors, the opportunities are growing.

From our experience, we recommend taking advantage of any occasion to get onto a sailboat and learn. The more you know about sailing, the more you'll enjoy being on the water. And that will make the sport better for everyone involved. Good luck.

Resources

There are many excellent resources available for those who would like to learn more about sailing. Here are some of the books, magazines, videotapes, and organizations that we recommend.

General

BOOKS

The Annapolis Book of Seamanship, 2nd ed., by John Rousmaniere (New York: Simon & Schuster, 1989). The authority on all aspects of sailing seamanship.

Piloting, Seamanship and Small Boat Handling, 58th ed., by Elbert S. Maloney (New York: Hearst Marine, 1987). Usually referred to as "Chapman's" (after its originator, Charles F. Chapman), this has long been the bible for seamanship and navigation.

North University Cruising Course (Milford, CT: North Sails, 1990). An authoritative manual on how to make your boat sail to its potential.

MAGAZINES

Sail (100 First Ave., Charlestown, MA 02129). Very good instructional articles for beginning and intermediate sailors and racers.

ORGANIZATIONS

United States Yacht Racing Union (USYRU). The governing body for the sport of sailing in the U.S. Anyone who wants to get more involved in sailing should become a member and take advantage of their many services and resources. Write to P.O. Box 209, Newport RI 02840 or call (401) 849-5200.

232

BOOKS

Precision Cruising by Arthur Chace (New York: Norton, 1987). An interesting collection of stories about how to cruise your boat "right."

MAGAZINES

Cruising World (John Clarke Rd., Newport, RI 02840). Good, general articles on all aspects of cruising.

Boardsailing

BOOKS

Sports Illustrated Boardsailing by Major Hall (New York: Sports Illustrated, 1985). The best how-to book on boardsailing, from the coach of the U.S. boardsailing team.

Racing

BOOKS AND MANUALS

1989–92 International Yacht Racing Rules. The text of the current racing rules. Available from USYRU, P.O. Box 209, Newport, RI 02840.

North U. Fast and *Smart Course* (Milford, Conn.: North Sails, 1988). These thick manuals are the authoritative references for learning about sail trim, rig tuning, boat handling, tactics, strategy, and much more.

Sailing Smart: Winning Techniques, Tactics and Strategy by Buddy Melges and Charles Mason (New York: Holt, 1983). How to win races according to the legendary "Wizard of Zenda."

Understanding the Yacht Racing Rules Through 1992, 2nd ed., by Dave Perry (New York: Putnam, 1989). A great explanation of the racing rules; the most highly regarded and widely read book among racing sailors.

Winning in One-Designs by Dave Perry (New York: Dodd, Mead, 1984). An excellent collection of articles on tactics and strategy that first appeared in *Sailing World* magazine.

MAGAZINES

Sailing World (5 John Clarke Rd., Newport, RI 02840). Excellent instructional articles for racing sailors.

VIDEOS

Learn the Racing Rules by Dave Dellenbaugh (New Haven: SEA-TV, 1989). A two-part video using both "live" boats and simulation to explain all the rules that racing sailors need to know.

Trim for Speed (North Sails/Henry English, 1990). A one-hour video from the world's leading sailmaker on how to trim your mainsail, genoa, and spinnaker.

ORGANIZATIONS

One Design Class Council. Almost every type of small racing sailboat has a national organization that can supply you with information about your boat. To find out how to get in touch with your class association, write to the council c/o USYRU, P.O. Box 209, Newport, RI 02840.

Reference

BOOKS

The Art and Science of Sails by Tom Whidden (New York: St. Martin's, 1990). A complete new reference on all aspects of sails and sailmaking, by the president of North Sails.

Sailing Theory and Practice by C. A. Marchaj (New York: Dodd, Mead, 1964). This has long been the authoritative reference for all aspects of technical sailing theory.

Glossary

A

Abeam. At right angles to the centerline of the boat.

Aft. Toward the stern.

Altocumulus clouds. A cloud formation (at about 20,000 feet) indicating the approach of a cold front.

Altostratus clouds. A continuous layer of clouds (at roughly 20,000 to 30,000 feet) that precedes a warm front.

Amidships. Toward the middle of the boat.

Anemometer. An instrument that measures the velocity of the wind.

Angle of attack. The angle between a sail and the wind or between a hydrofoil and the water flow.

Angle of sail. The angle between the boat's compass course and the true wind direction.

Apparent wind. The wind you feel on a moving boat.

Astern. Toward or at the back of the boat; behind the boat.

Athwartships. In a direction perpendicular to the boat's centerline; from side to side.

B

Back. (v) To trim a sail on the windward side; (n.) a wind shift in a counter-clockwise direction.

Backstay. A wire that runs from the stern to the top of the mast, used to control mast bend.

Backwind. The disturbed air flow that exists to leeward of any sailboat, also called bad air, dirty air, wind shadow, wind blanket.

Barberhauler. A line-and-block system used to move the jib lead outboard.

Battens. Long, thin, narrow pieces of fiberglass or wood that fit in pockets on the leech of the mainsail and support the aft part of the sail.

Beam. The maximum width of a boat.

Beam reach. The point of sail with the wind blowing at 90 degrees to the boat's heading.

Bear off. To turn the boat away from the wind (opposite of *luff*).

Beat. (v) To sail upwind; (n) any leg of a race on which you must sail upwind.

Beaufort scale. A system for describing wind velocity.

Block. A pulley used for turning line.

Boom. The spar to which the foot of the mainsail is attached.

Boom vang. A mechanical system used to keep the boom from lifting.

Bow. The pointy end of the boat; the front of the boat.

Bowline. The most important knot for sailors to know.

Broach. What happens when a boat sailing downwind in heavy air loses steering control and rounds up toward the wind.

Broad reach. Sailing offwind with the wind direction at an angle of roughly 120 to 160 degrees to the bow.

By-the-lee. Sailing downwind with the wind blowing from the leeward side of the transom.

C

Cam cleat. A fitting that uses interlocking teeth on springs *(cams)* to hold the line.

Capsize. To tip over.

Catamaran. A boat with two hulls.

Catboat. A sailboat that has a mainsail only.

Centerboard. A wood, fiberglass, or metal hydrofoil that pivots on a pin in the middle of the boat, used to keep the boat from going sideways when sailing upwind.

Centerline. The (imaginary) line that runs down the center of the boat, from stern to bow.

Chine. The line where the sides of a boat intersect the boat's bottom.

Chop. Short, irregular waves.

Chord. An imaginary line drawn between the luff and leech of a sail and parallel to the water surface, used for describing sail shape.

Chute. Another name for a spinnaker (from "parachute").

Cirrus clouds. A high, wispy cloud formation that provides the first warning of an oncoming warm front.

Clam cleat. A metal or plastic cleat with jaws fixed in a vertical plane.

Cleat. A device used for securing a line.

Clew. The lower, aft corner of a sail.

Close-hauled. Sailing as close to the wind as you can in order to make progress upwind.

Close reach. The point of sail between close-hauled and beam reaching.

Coaming. The raised protection around a cockpit.

Cockpit. The area of a boat where the crew sits.

COLREGS. The international rules of the road; these apply to outer coastal waters and the high seas.

Compass. A magnetized card that indicates direction relative to magnetic north.

Cover. In racing, to stay between your opponents astern and the next mark.

Cumulonimbus clouds. High, powerful thunderstorm clouds.

Cumulus clouds. The fair-weather cloud, characterized by its puffy white appearance.

Cunningham. The line that controls the luff tension of a mainsail; also called a *downhaul*.

Current. Horizontal movement of water.

D

Daggerboard. A hydrofoil that slides up and down in the center of the boat.

Depower. To reduce heeling force by altering sail trim.

Displacement. The weight of water displaced by a boat.

Downhaul. A line used to hold down a mast or the bottom of a sail; also called a *cunningham*.

Downwind. Away from the wind; sailing with the wind behind.

Draft. The distance from the water surface to the bottom of a boat's keel or centerboard.

Drag. Resistance caused by wind and water.

Dry suit. A protective one-piece suit that has seals at the wrists, ankles, and neck to keep the wearer dry.

E

Ease. To let out a sheet.

Ebb. The outgoing tide.

F

Figure-eight knot. A knot shaped like an 8, used in the end of a line, such as a jib sheet, to keep it from pulling through a block.

Flake. To fold the sails in place on the boat.

Flood. The incoming tide.

Fly. A type of wind vane, attached to the top of the mast.

Foot. (n) The bottom edge of a sail; (v) when sailing upwind, to ease the sheets slightly and sail fast instead of trying to point.

Fore and aft. In a direction parallel to the centerline of the boat.

Foreguy. The line that's used to keep the spinnaker pole from going up in the air.

Forestay. The wire stay running from the bow to the mast, on which the jib is set (also called the *headstay*).

Forward. Toward the bow.

Fractional rig. A rig where the forestay doesn't go all the way to the top of the mast.

Front. The approaching edge of a new weather system.

Furl. To roll up the mainsail tightly on the boom.

G

Genoa. A large jib that overlaps the forward part of the mainsail.

Gooseneck. The swivel fitting that attaches the boom to the mast.

Groove. When sailing upwind, you are said to be "in the groove" when the boat feels good and is going fast.

Gudgeon. Metal fitting on the transom into which the rudder pintle is inserted.

Gunwale. (Pronounced like *tunnel.*) The rail of the boat at deck level.

Guy. The spinnaker sheet on the windward side; the guy always goes through the outboard end of the spinnaker pole.

Guy hook. A metal hook near the shrouds, used to keep the guy from flying up in the air.

H

Halyard. The line or wire used to raise a sail.

Handicap. A type of racing among dissimilar boats where final positions are determined by the boats' measured ratings.

Head. The boat's toilet; the top corner of a sail.

Header. A wind shift toward the bow, forcing you to head off.

Head to wind. The position of a boat when her bow is pointing into the wind.

Heavy air. Windy conditions.

Heel. To tip to one side.

Helm. The rudder and tiller, and the feeling they generate.

Helmsperson. The person who is steering the boat.

Hike. To sit on the windward side of the boat and lean out to keep the boat flat when it's windy.

Hiking stick. An extension attached to the end of the tiller that allows the helmsperson to hike while he or she is steering.

Hiking strap. A strap fastened in the cockpit so a crew member can hook his or her feet under it and hike out.

Hull. The main body of a boat.

Hyperpyrexia. Heat stress, caused by high temperatures, humidity, sun exposure, and exercise.

Hypothermia. A dangerous condition brought on by overexposure to cold.

I

Iceboat. A boat with metal blades that sails on ice and goes very fast.

Inland Rules. The Inland Navigational Rules of the United States; these apply to lakes, rivers, and nearby coastal waters.

Irons. A boat is said to be "in irons" when it is stuck head to wind with no steerageway.

J

Jib. The small triangular sail that sets in front of the mainsail.

Jibe. To go from one tack to the other by turning the boat so the stern passes through the wind.

K

Keel. A heavy, deep hydrofoil that sticks down under a boat and helps the boat sail to windward as well as reduce heel.

Kite. Another name for a spinnaker.

Knot. One nautical mile (6,080 feet) per hour.

L

Lay line. An imaginary line on which a boat can sail close-hauled and just clear a mark or obstruction.

Leech. The aft edge of a sail.

Leeward. (Pronounced *loo-ard*.) The side of the boat that's away from the wind; the side where the boom is.

Leeway. The drift that a sailboat makes to leeward when sailing upwind.

Lift. A wind shift away from the bow, allowing the boat to head up; a beneficial aerodynamic and hydrodynamic force.

Light air. Calm conditions, light breezes.

Line. A rope.

Luff. (n) The forward edge of any sail; the action of the sails as they flap in the breeze; (v) to turn the boat toward the wind (the opposite of *bear off*).

Lull. A temporary calm in the wind.

M

Mainsail. The sail that is set on the mast and boom.

Mainsheet. The line that controls the trim of the mainsail.

Mark. A buoy or any other object that a racing boat must leave on a designated side.

Mast. The vertical spar that supports the sails.

N

NOAA. The National Oceanic and Atmospheric Administration.

O

Offshore breeze. A breeze that is blowing away from the land, toward the water.

One-design. Any sailboat that is part of a class where the rules require that all boats are the same.

Ooch. Sudden forward and aft body movement, to initiate surfing or planing.

Oscillating breeze. A wind that shifts back and forth; also called a *phasing breeze.*

Outboard. Outward from the hull.

Outhaul. The line system that is used to pull the clew of the mainsail toward the end of the boom.

Overpowered. Heeling too much.

Overstand. In racing, to sail beyond the lay lines to the windward mark.

Overtake. To catch another boat from astern.

P

Partners. The opening where the mast goes through the deck.

Persistent shift. What happens when the wind shifts continuously in a clockwise or counterclockwise direction.

PFD. Personal flotation device; also called a *life jacket.*

Pinching. When sailing upwind, heading the boat a little higher than normal so the front of the jib begins to luff.

Pintle. A metal pin attached to the leading edge of the rudder; it fits into a gudgeon on the transom.

Planing. When a boat, usually on a reach, goes fast enough to ride on top of the water.

Points of sail. The direction of the boat in relation to the wind, including beating, reaching, and running.

Polypropylene. A clothing material usually worn as an inner layer for warmth and to "wick" water away from the skin.

Port. The left side of the boat as you look toward the bow.

Puff. A temporary gust of wind.

Pump. Rapid trimming and releasing of a sail to gain a burst of speed.

R

Racing rules. A set of rules, published by the International Yacht Racing Union, that govern yacht racing around the world.

Rake. The fore and aft tilt of a mast away from vertical (usually aft).

Ratchet block. A block that turns in one direction only, making it easier to hold a line under tension.

Reach. To sail with the wind blowing from the beam.

Ready about. An expression, usually used by the helmsperson, that alerts the crew to an upcoming tack.

Rhumb line. The straight sailing course between any two points or marks.

Roach. The area of a mainsail aft of a straight line between head and clew.

Roll tack. Aggressive use of crew weight during a tack.

Rub rail. An extra protective railing at the gunwale.

Rudder. The hydrofoil at the stern of the boat, used for steering.

Running. Sailing with the wind from astern.

S

Sailboard. A flat-hulled boat with a mainsail; looks like a surfboard with a sail.

Scull. To propel the boat by moving the rudder back and forth sharply.

Sheave. The wheel or roller that's inside a block.

Sheet. A line that is used to trim a sail.

Shroud. The wire stays on each side of the boat.

Skeg. A small, fixed fin on the bottom of the boat just forward of the rudder.

Sloop. A sailboat that has one mast with a main and a jib.

Spar. A generic name for the poles that support the sails—mast, boom, and spinnaker pole.

Spinnaker. The large, round, colorful sail, usually made of nylon, that is used when sailing downwind.

Splash rail. A protective railing on the deck, just forward of the cockpit, used to keep water out of the cockpit.

Spreader. A horizontal strut on the mast, to which shrouds are attached.

Starboard. The right side of the boat as you look toward the bow.

Stays. Wires that support the mast: *shrouds, forestay, backstay*.

Steerageway. Enough speed to allow a boat to respond to the movement of the rudder.

Stem. The point where the topsides meet at the bow.

Stern. The back end of the boat.

Strategy. An overall game plan for how to use the wind, waves, and current to get around the race course as fast as possible.

Surfing. The action of a boat, sailing downwind, as it accelerates down the face of a wave.

T

Tack. (n) The forward, lower corner of a sail; the direction a boat is moving relative to the wind (on a *starboard tack*); (v) to change from one tack to another by turning the boat so the bow moves through the wind.

Tactics. The moves you make relative to other boats that help you follow your race strategy.

Takedown. The act of lowering the spinnaker; also called *dousing* or *dropping*.

Telltale. A piece of yarn on the shrouds or sails used to show the direction of the wind or air flow.

Tide. The up and down movement of large bodies of water, caused by the moon.

Tiller. A straight piece of wood or metal that's attached to the top of the rudder and is used for steering.

Topping lift. The halyard that's used to hold up the spinnaker pole.

Topsides. The side of a boat, between the waterline and the gunwale.

Towline. A line by which a boat can be towed.

Transom. The part of the hull, at the stern, that faces aft.

Trapeze. A wire system used to let a crew member stand straight out from the side of the boat in heavy wind.

Traveler. Usually a car-and-track arrangement, near the middle or stern of the boat, that controls the position of the boom.

Trim. To pull a sail in tighter by pulling on the sheet.

True wind. The wind felt by a person on a stationary object such as the shore or an anchored boat.

Tuning. The fine art of adjusting your mast and shrouds to make the boat go fast.

Turtle. The bag or box from which you set the spinnaker; upside down: a capsized boat with its mast sticking straight down is said to have *turtled*.

Twing. A short line on each side of the boat used to keep the spinnaker sheets under control.

Twist. The amount that the leech of a sail falls off to leeward.

U

Upwind. Toward or into the wind.

USYRU. The United States Yacht Racing Union, which governs all sailboat racing in the U.S.

V

Veer. A clockwise wind shift.

W

Waterline. The part of the hull at the surface of the water, often indicated by a stripe.

Weather. Often used in place of *windward;* for example, *weather mark* or *weather helm.*

Whisker pole. A lightweight spar used to hold out the jib when sailing downwind without a spinnaker.

Wind shadow. The turbulent air to leeward of a sail.

Windsurfer®. The original and most popular brand of sailboard.

Windward. The side of the boat toward the wind; the side opposite the boom.

Windward helm. The tendency of a boat to turn to windward when you let go of the tiller.

Wing and wing. Sailing downwind with the jib filled on the opposite side of the main.